"Dena Dyer writes this encouraging devotional with vulnerability and wisdom, which will refresh the hearts of busy moms in whatever season of life they find themselves."

—CHERI FULLER, speaker and author
of the best-selling *When Mothers Pray*
and *The Mom You're Meant to Be*

"As a mother of seven, I appreciate a book that allows me to escape the hectic pace of motherhood and take an oasis break for a moment or two. Dena Dyer has created a delightful haven with words for busy moms. I highly recommend this wonderful book. In one gentle stroke, it will lighten your load, rejuvenate your sense of fun, and refresh your spirit."

—ELLIE KAY, "America's Financial Expert"
and author of eight books including
A Woman's Guide to Family Finance

"Dena Dyer's *Grace for the Race* reminds me of Anne Morrow Lindbergh's *Gifts from the Sea*. I love Dena's poignant reflections."

—MARSHA MARKS, author of
*If I Ignore It, It Will Go Away,
and Other Lies I Thought Were True*

"Dena Dyer is a young mother who 'tells it like it is'—often harried, often hilarious, and often awesome. Her 'Notes from the Coach' after each devotional provide a grand finale for the daily message. The scriptures she cites are right on and speak from the printed page with just the message needed for the day."

—RUTHIE ARNOLD, coauthor of
Help! I'm Turning into My Mother
and the best-selling
Worms in My Tea and Other Mixed Blessings

Grace FOR THE Race

MEDITATIONS FOR BUSY MOMS

by Dena Dyer

BARBOUR
PUBLISHING

Cover design and illustration: Greg Jackson, Jackson Design Co, LLC

Published by Barbour Publishing, Inc., P.O. Box 719, Uhrichsville, Ohio 44683, www.barbourbooks.com

Our mission is to publish and distribute inspirational products offering exceptional value and biblical encouragement to the masses.

Member of the
Evangelical Christian
Publishers Association

Printed in the United States of America.
5 4 3 2 1

Dedication

For Carey

Acknowledgments

A first book is always a group project. I could never have written this volume by myself—especially since I was pregnant with my second son as I was completing it!

So I want to thank all the people who inspired and helped me:

- My husband, Carey Dyer, for always believing in me and for being my first editor.

- My son, Jordan, for all the great material and for saying, "You don't have to ask, Mommy, just go ahead!" when I asked for permission to write about him.

- My parents, Rayford and Susie Ratliff, for all the countless hours and dollars they've spent encouraging my writing (from second grade on!) through books bought, conferences paid for, and articles read. Thanks, Dad, for saying, "You're already a successful writer!" when I despaired of ever getting a book contract.

- My agent, Frank Weimann. Thanks for all your work and advice on my behalf! I'm proud to be associated with you.

- The Granbury Live family. Thanks for being my cheerleaders and confidantes, and for supporting my writing dreams, even when it took me away from our ministry together.

- My good friends in Granbury and the members of Lakeside Baptist Church. I'm blessed to be associated with such dynamic, godly people.

And, of course, to my writing mentors and friends:

- Florence and Marita Littauer and the whole CLASS staff (Craig, Linda, Lauren, and all the others) who helped me hone my craft, understand my calling, and expand my circle of contacts.

- Ruthie Arnold—thank you for all the lunches at the Merry Heart Tea Room and for introducing me to many new friends in the writing world. You're a role model and an inspiration!

- Robert Darden, my Baylor writing instructor. Thanks for the example and the instruction.

- Karen O'Connor, Becky Freeman, Ellie Kay, Lee Hough, Ken Gire, Karol Ladd, Allison Gappa-Bottke, and Gracie Arnold—for encouragement, critiques, and realistic (but upbeat) analysis of what it takes to "make it" in this crazy business.

- Leigh Anne Jasheway—for the comedic "tweaking" you did on my proposal. It worked!

- Laurie Copeland—for helping me write "1 Corinthians 13 for Busy Moms" and "Falling into Grace," and for letting me tell her story in "Out of the Mouths of Babes." I love your sense of humor, you groovy chick!

- The Fellowship of Christian Writers (my local and online group, and the Tulsa gang). You've all been a godsend!

Contents

Introduction

I'm so honored that you've picked up this book! It's my hope that through the real-life anecdotes in *Grace for the Race*, you will realize that God doesn't desire perfection. What He does desire is daily surrender of our expectations, schedules, emotions, and relationships.

By being honest and vulnerable about the ways God has shown Himself to me as I've struggled with motherhood, I hope to help you realize that you're not alone—and you're not crazy! I surely don't have it all together (in fact, I usually can't even *find* it all), but I do have a Coach who holds me together.

And I long to come alongside you as a fellow runner, not an expert, to cheer you on in your daily race. Simply put, I wanted to write a book for moms that I would buy, read, recommend, and give away—one that is biblically based, humorous, helpful, and hopeful. I also wanted to write short meditations that you could read quickly, in those few stolen moments we moms have!

Grace for the Race is divided into nine sections. Each piece begins with a thought-provoking and/or humorous quote and ends with "Notes from the Coach," encouraging scriptures related to the meditation. You can read them in order or pick the sections that pertain to your life right now.

Training Well features pieces related to my growing years and how the things I absorbed influence my parenting (in both good and bad ways). I hope to convince you that viewing our childhoods—even the unsavory parts—through the lens of God's grace can help us become better parents.

Warming Up and Stretching Out is about accepting our weaknesses—and our children's—as gifts from God. Hopefully, He can use our faults to make us more compassionate.

The First Lap is all about the first few sleep-deprived, *insane* years of parenthood. They show us our need for God and His gentle care for us as His children.

In **Using Proper Equipment**, I deal with the fact that we moms need prayer, wisdom, a sense of humor, a godly church family, and supportive friends to make it through parenting with our wits and self-esteem intact. (We also may need a counselor on speed-dial!)

My goal with **Hopping Over the Hurdles** is to encourage you to let God remove the peace-blocking obstacles of perfectionism, competitiveness, unrealistic expectations, packed schedules, and impatience from your life.

Handing It Off deals with the fact that life is not a solo race—it's a relay. I want to help you contemplate the value of reaching out to others and being gentle with yourself during tough times.

As the race becomes difficult, we moms tend to feel alone and lost. **In the Final Stretch** shows how God can help us "kick it out" and reach reserves of strength and wisdom we never knew we had—if we ask Him to.

Paul tells us in 1 Corinthians 9 that we must run the race as if our life depended on it—and, come to think of it, it does! And if we've received abundant life, shouldn't we share it? The devotionals in **Crossing the Finish Line** are meant to help you recognize your place in the race (and God's offer of peace in the midst of storms).

And finally, **On the Podium** celebrates several gifts of grace—husbands, children, fulfilling work, godly ancestors, and faith.

So there you have it. I hope you enjoy *Grace for the Race*—and I'm praying that God will use this book to show you His love for you. If we hold fast to Him, He will be there at the finish line saying, "Well done, My good and faithful servant."

And that's worth its weight in gold.

Give me your grace,

most loving Jesus,

and I will run after You

to the finish line, forever.

Help me, Jesus,

because I want to do this

with burning fervor,

speedily.

SAINT FRANCES CABRINI

SECTION ONE

Training Well

What Mom Taught Me

An ounce of mother is worth a pound of clergy.

RUDYARD KIPLING

Bless her heart, my mom really tried to teach me the domestic necessities of life. After all, she was an interior designer in college. She must be so ashamed—I can't even sew the simplest thing. (All hail the Buttoneer!)

And as hard as she tried to teach me to cook, just last night I messed up again in the kitchen. My darling hubby Carey (who usually makes meals for us—PTL!) was gone to the store for a couple of items. When he came back in and looked at the stove, he sighed. "Sweetheart," he said, with just a tinge of frustration, "you're supposed to brown the meat and *then* put the taco seasoning on it." Oops!

Other goofs I've made in the culinary department are legendary. Don't even think of asking my brother about the oatmeal bricks—ahem, cookies—I made when we were teenagers. I thought it said three cups of flour instead of one—honest mistake! And then there was "Quichegate," when I embarrassed my spouse at a party we threw for fellow youth workers. After we cooked the quiche, Carey discovered that I had poured the liquid egg and cheese mixture over the ready-made crust without taking the crust's paper liner off first.

But all is not lost—my mom did teach me a lot.

Mom never ran a marathon—but she ran to the store at

midnight for medicine for me. She never held public office—but she knocked on doors so Dad could win his race as county judge.

Mom gave up her dream of writing when she bore two children within eighteen months, but she's the first person to squeal when I report good news about my freelance career. She never climbed the corporate ladder—but she climbed into the tree house with me for teddy bear picnics.

Mom never worked outside the home, but she always worked at making the inside of our home an oasis.

These are things she *has* done: dried hundreds of my tears when I had boy troubles, slept on the foot of my twin bed when I had nightmares, traveled to nearly all of my singing performances, and prayed thousands of prayers for me. (I laugh about it, but it's true—when I want a prayer answered quickly, I tell Mom. She seems to have a red phone to the Great Throne.)

Since I've been an adult, Mom has become more of a friend and confidant to me than ever before. I've told her many times that she is my hero—especially since I had my son, and I realized the heartache and sleepless nights I put her through!

So, Mom—I didn't learn to cook or sew, as hard as you tried to teach me. But I did learn from your example that children are a gift from God, and time with them is worth sacrificing for.

And thanks for praying for a husband for me—who can cook!

NOTES FROM THE COACH

Her children arise and call her blessed;
her husband also, and he praises her.

PROVERBS 31:28 NIV

The sayings of King Lemuel—
an oracle his mother taught him...

PROVERBS 31:1 NIV (EMPHASIS ADDED)

That precious memory triggers another:
your honest faith—and what a rich faith it is,
handed down from your grandmother Lois
to your mother Eunice, and now to you!

2 TIMOTHY 1:5 MSG

Coming Home

Women who are brought up in the country
are stronger than men who live in towns.

SAINT JOHN CHRYSOSTOM

I've had a few unpleasant jobs in my life—telemarketing being one of them. I also filled in for my dad's legal secretary a few times, which was more boring than hard. But for backbreaking work, nothing beats the summers I rounded up cattle on horseback and cleaned out smelly stock trailers on our family ranch. It wasn't my idea of fun—but my dad insisted we learn the responsibility that went along with the rewards of country living.

While my friends sunbathed as lifeguards and helped customers in air-conditioned clothing shops in our small Texas town, I grumbled and complained my way through six summers of ranch work.

I can remember telling my parents I couldn't wait to leave the ranch and our small town. I felt confined, stifled, and restless. There was so much more to do and see than tend cattle and watch seedlings grow. "When I grow up, I'm going to live in a city apartment and have a window box," I said to my mom more than once.

Recently, Carey and I took our towheaded son Jordan to Hay Creek Ranch, as my parents named it. The meadow grass was green from spring rains, and the homeplace had never looked more beautiful.

Jordan had quite a time seeing the cows, playing on the fort, and navigating the now-rusty slide that Dad had built for my brother and me twenty-five years ago. I enjoyed hearing Mom tell Carey how her granddaddy had traded a horse and saddle for our seven-hundred-acre spread. On a cow-checking trip in my parents' beat-up Suburban, we saw deer, pheasant, cottontail rabbits, quail, and windmills. Jordan had two words for it all—"Oh, wow!"

Jordy went on walks with my parents, where he chased the gentle cattle and ran from our overly friendly ranch dogs. He fed the horses with Dad and tried on the miniature vest and chaps that Mom had sewed for him, grinning all the while.

And when Carey and I took a walk one afternoon, I proudly pointed out the trees I had helped plant with my sibling's help. The once-small seedlings now grew tall and strong, providing shade around the fence near the house.

I thought about where we live now—in a small Texas town, not unlike the one I grew up in. We live in a four-bedroom "ranch-style" house with a big yard, and we've been poring over gardening and landscape magazines. I want to plant trees, build a playhouse for Jordan, and have a garden that attracts bunnies and birds.

Proverbs 22:6 (NIV) says, "Train a child in the way he should go, and when he is old he will not turn from it."

Now, in my thirties, I realize the excellent training my parents gave me, and I appreciate the faith and values that they tirelessly modeled. Those are the things that made me who I am, now that I'm grown up. And those are things I want to pass on.

NOTES FROM THE COACH

Pay close attention, friend, to what your father tells you;
never forget what you learned at your mother's knee.

PROVERBS 1:8 MSG

Impress [the commandments] on your children.
Talk about them when you sit at home
and when you walk along the road,
when you lie down and when you get up.

DEUTERONOMY 6:7 NIV

The LORD's curse is on the house of the wicked,
but he blesses the home of the righteous.

PROVERBS 3:33 NIV

A person who strays from home is like
a bird that strays from its nest.

PROVERBS 27:8 NLT

"On that day I will gather you together
and bring you home again."

ZEPHANIAH 3:20 NLT

What Real Love Looks Like

Now I know what love is.

VIRGIL

My firstborn made my day—no, my decade—recently when we were licking ice cream cones at Sonic with his dad, Carey. (Every so often, we visit the king of drive-in milk shakes and burgers, in our pajamas. It's a quirky family tradition.) Nonchalantly, I asked five-year-old Jordan whom he would marry if he could choose right now. Carey rolled his eyes, because he doesn't understand the motherly need for affirmation— yea verily, even worship—from the fruit of our labor.

Without hesitation, Jordan said, "You."

I melted faster than a soft-serve cone in the Texas heat.

I know Jordan's hero worship of me won't last forever. In fact, I knew it on the day we brought him home from the hospital. In a fit of hormonal fluctuation, I lay on the couch crying, with my firstborn on my tummy.

"What's wrong?" asked Carey.

"He's going to grow up and leave me for another woman," I sobbed. Again, Carey rolled his eyes.

But you, dear readers, understand.

You understand that never in our lives B.K. (before kids) had we experienced such passionate, fervent love for someone.

And in the B.K. years, we simply couldn't imagine that their unconditional acceptance would transform us even more than the changes wrought by romantic love.

To tell the truth, I was a very late bloomer in the love game.

In first grade, my friends and I played catch-'em-and-kiss-'em on the playground, and the girls won. I kissed a boy named Robbie, and he said, "Yuck."

In eighth grade, a dark-headed Italian freshman I met at summer church camp held my hand after a bus ride. I wrote—he never wrote back.

In college, a guy whose name I can't remember asked me out to a freshman dance and then wanted to marry me. It was my turn to say, "Yuck."

The next guy I dated dumped me for another girl when I went home for the weekend. And the only serious boyfriend I ever had told me after two years together that he was considering an "alternative lifestyle."

It wasn't until after college that I met Carey, my soul mate. Many of my friends were already married when we said, "I do." But I wouldn't trade the wait for anything.

Through many ups and downs, God taught me to stop running after false love and from His real love. I learned to bask in the light of God's Son until I felt loved enough to not care as much whether a human being thought I was good-looking, talented, or smart. I learned (from wise teachers, godly counselors, and hard life experience) to wait for the best instead of settling for average.

Frederick Buechner once wrote, "Life itself is grace." I believe that love itself is grace, too—the kind of love that says hello with slobbery kisses and gifts of crumpled wildflowers, that asks for one more story—"Tree Pigs, 'gin, Mama"—and hides Cheerios in the sofa when you aren't looking.

This kind of love holds the wastebasket under my head all night on Valentine's Day after I've had some bad pasta.

This kind of loves perseveres even in the face of competition from our kids, careers, and culture.

And this kind of love celebrates—with minimal eye-rolling—small miracles, like pajama-clad declarations of devotion, offered with a pure heart and sticky hands.

NOTES FROM THE COACH

Love is patient, love is kind. It does not envy,
it does not boast, it is not proud.
It is not rude, it is not self-seeking,
it is not easily angered, it keeps no record of wrongs.
Love does not delight in evil but rejoices with the truth.
It always protects, always trusts,
always hopes, always perseveres.

1 CORINTHIANS 13:4–7 NIV

Place me like a seal over your heart,
like a seal on your arm;
for love is as strong as death,
its jealousy unyielding as the grave.
It burns like a blazing fire, like a mighty flame.
Many waters cannot quench love;
rivers cannot wash it away.
If one were to give all the wealth of his house for love,
it would be utterly scorned.

SONG OF SONGS 8:6–7 NIV

Red Doors

*Most women put off entertaining
until the kids are grown.*

ERMA BOMBECK

I love red doors. I always have. They say to me: "This is a fun place. Come on in." Red doors are welcoming, comforting, and unique.

Maybe one of the reasons I love them is that my grandmother had a red front door.

Nanaw, like her door, was welcoming, comforting, and unique. Her house was filled with mismatched furniture—a bright blue cabinet here, a red couch there. But somehow, it all worked. Once, she gave me a green skirt with pink frogs on it. I never wore it and joked with my mother about Nanaw's lack of "taste," but I wish I hadn't given it away.

At eighty-two, my art-teacher/Realtor grandmother learned to use the computer for the first time, and she wrote and self-published a beautiful book (*Times Was*) about growing up during the Depression.

And every Wednesday night when I was in elementary school, Nanaw babysat my brother and me while our parents were at church choir practice. She fed us cookies, sodas, and taught us card games like poker and blackjack. (To my father's disgust, she would never let us win—we had to earn it!)

I miss her a lot. While going through Nanaw's things after

her funeral, I kept a blue cabinet and red couch. Somehow, they work really well together in my home. And when I came across her perfumes, I realized with a smile that one of her favorites was Red Door by Elizabeth Arden! I took a partially full bottle home with me and used it for months.

I think I'm a lot like Nanaw, or at least I hope so. I also hope that people see me—and my home—as welcoming, comforting, and unique. It makes me wonder: Is the door of my heart painted red? If I have Jesus in my heart, shouldn't it be a place of joy, compassion, and creativity? Do people—especially Jesus—find my home (and my heart) a hospitable place?

For a period of two years, a group of neighborhood children seemed to spend more time at my house than at their own. They played in the front yard, the backyard, my son's room, and the living room. They made messes, ate cookies by the handful, and generally wreaked havoc in our little abode.

At the time, I complained about the lack of supervision (and food) their parents provided. But I sometimes miss them since they moved away. And, looking back, I'm honored that they felt comfortable enough in my home that when I opened the door, they came right on in—whether I wanted them to or not!

Now, two houses are going up in the neighborhood, and I hope the families that move into them have lots of kids.

Recently, I painted my front door red. And I'm going to start looking for new cookie recipes and stocking up on Kool-Aid.

I think Nanaw—and Jesus—would be proud.

NOTES FROM THE COACH

[Jesus said,] "Here I am!
I stand at the door and knock.
If anyone hears my voice and opens the door,
I will come in and eat with him, and he with me."

REVELATION 3:20 NIV

Help needy Christians; be inventive in hospitality.

ROMANS 12:13 MSG

Do not forget to entertain strangers,
for by so doing some people have
entertained angels without knowing it.

HEBREWS 13:2 NIV

Cheerfully share your home with those who
need a meal or a place to stay.

1 PETER 4:9 NLT

Dear friend, when you extend hospitality to
Christian brothers and sisters,
even when they are strangers, you make the faith visible.

3 JOHN 5 MSG

Hiding in Plain Sight

*Eddie admitted that some of his life
he'd spent hiding from God,
and the rest of the time he thought he went unnoticed.*

MITCH ALBOM

I've never been in the trouble with the law, unless you count getting stopped by lenient highway patrolmen several times during my college years. Never mind that I had a lead foot; I think I was being profiled (blond young woman + red car = you get the picture).

What infuriates my husband is that I always got off with just a warning. (The tears, plus my unnerving honesty—"But, Officer, I had to go to the bathroom really bad!"—helped.) It probably also didn't hurt that my father was a county attorney, and a sticker displaying his logo was featured prominently on my front windshield.

Carey, on the other hand, has been stopped only twice in his life, and he got a ticket—for going too slow. Seriously. But that's another story for another day.

Besides the struggle with keeping my car under the posted speed limits, my teenage years were far from eventful. Only once or twice did I play with fire.

One Friday night, I got in the car with two of my high school girlfriends and went to Sunray, a neighboring town, without telling my parents. Not only that, but my buddies saw some young men they knew and invited the guys to hop in the car. So there I was, cavorting in a car with strange young men. I was scared that my father would find out, so I decided to use an alias.

Jennifer Garner I was not. When the boys in the car asked my name, I squeaked out, "Elizabeth Kumquat," or something equally unbelievable. My girlfriends' eyes got wide, and they stifled laughter. But the guys weren't paying attention to me— they were too into the evening's gossip.

"Did you see Dena out tonight?" said one.

My heart stopped.

"Dena Ratliff?" asked the other.

I almost fainted. (Ratliff was my maiden name.)

"No, stupid, Deana Miller. Dena Ratliff wouldn't be driving around. She's too square!"

Relieved beyond belief, I said a hearty, "Amen!"

What a silly girl I was—hiding in plain sight. And, now that I think about it, I was stupid for getting in a car with people I didn't know. The story scares me a little, but it also shows me that God has a sense of humor. He knew where I was, even if my parents didn't. And He didn't let me forget it.

Since then, I've hidden in plain sight many times.

I've stayed busy with "holy" activities while neglecting my personal time with God. I've gone shopping when I should have confronted a friend about a spiritual issue. I've yelled at my kids when I could have prayed for patience and taken a time-out for Mommy.

But God always knows where I am—and, more importantly, He sees the reasons (fear, bitterness, confusion, doubt) I'm hiding.

Through my pain, He says, "Come out, come out, wherever you are! I long to heal you. Let's get through this together."

And when I finally answer, "Here I am," He runs to me with open arms.

Notes from the Coach

*But the L*ORD* God called to the man,*
"Where are you?"

G*ENESIS* 3:9 N*IV*

"But I have stripped Esau bare,
I have uncovered his hiding places
so that he will not be able to conceal himself."

J*EREMIAH* 49:10 N*ASB*

But you'll welcome us with open arms
when we run for cover to you.

P*SALM* 5:11 M*SG*

You are my hiding place;
You preserve me from trouble;
You surround me with songs of deliverance.

P*SALM* 32:7 N*ASB*

"Can a man hide himself in hiding places
*so I do not see him?" declares the L*ORD.
"Do I not fill the heavens and the earth?"

J*EREMIAH* 23:24 N*ASB*

SECTION TWO

Warming Up and Stretching Out

Sowing in Tears

*Perhaps our eyes need to be washed
by our tears once in a while,
so that we can see life with a clearer view again.*

ALEX TAN

My first pregnancy changed everything—my shoe size, contacts prescription, dress size, and my priorities. And as the mother of a newborn diagnosed with reflux, *I* changed everything, too (sheets, clothing, diapers, pillowcases)—often three times a day.

So it shouldn't have come as a surprise to me that pregnancy and childbirth would also alter my emotional makeup. But, as all women know, having a child also gives you a bad case of DMC (Diminished Mental Capacity). So I simply wasn't prepared.

It was December 1997. With a pillow on top of my pregnant belly and my swollen feet propped on the coffee table, I watched a television special on the most amazing moments of the year. As a picture of the McCaughey septuplets flashed on the screen, underscored by "The Circle of Life" from *The Lion King*, I bawled like a baby. That's when it hit me—something in me had definitely changed.

For most of my life, I had watched television shows, listened to music, and worshipped the Lord without even tearing up. Now I blubbered endlessly at anything remotely sentimental. Why the change? It was probably a combination of hormones, life experiences, and the realization that life is uncertain—and yet, often wonderful.

Growing up, I saw tears as a weakness. They simply weren't normal or healthy. And my consistent crying during pregnancy confused (and yes, I admit it) frustrated me.

However, today—six years later and pregnant again with my second child—I'm weeping freely. I now know that tears are as necessary as breathing, eating, and sleeping.

After all, Jesus cried at Jerusalem's shortsightedness, wept over the loss of Mary and Martha's brother, and sobbed with trepidation in the garden over His own excruciating future. And He's the strongest man I know.

He is also the wisest. "Keep me away from the wisdom which does not cry," said Kahlil Gibran.

In fact, an inability to weep is often cited as a symptom of depression. Don't you feel much better after a good cry? That's the way our Maker intended it. It's one of the biblical paradoxes that are more than true: Only when we allow ourselves to become broken will we be made whole.

The other day, my hubby and I were heatedly discussing finances, and the waterworks began in earnest. "Can I get you something?" he asked. "Tissues? A glass of water? Prozac?"

I laughed through my tears and said, "No. Just let me cry. I'll feel better."

Writer Ken Gire says: "In each tear is distilled something of eternity, something of love and compassion and tenderness, all things that originate in heaven and come to earth as a sacrament to my soul, if only I am willing to take and eat."

So whether I weep at a wedding, sob during a funeral, or tear up with joy while listening to a friend's good fortune, I'm no longer ashamed. In fact, during this pregnancy, I'm crying with abandon—content in the knowledge that I'm touching both heaven and earth at the same time.

Notes from the Coach

Those who sow in tears will reap with songs of joy.

PSALM 126:5 NIV

"This is what the LORD,
the God of your father David, says:
I have heard your prayer
and seen your tears; I will heal you."

2 KINGS 20:5 NIV

"My eyes pour out tears to God."

JOB 16:20 NIV

I am weary with my groaning;
Every night…I water my couch with my tears.

PSALM 6:6 ASV

You have seen me tossing and turning through the night.
You have collected all my tears
and preserved them in your bottle!
You have recorded every one in your book.

PSALM 56:8 TLB

Do You Think I'm Insecure?

*Self-respect is
the cornerstone
of all virtue.*

JOHN HERSCHEL

I usually feel pretty good about myself when I wake up—for the five minutes I refrain from looking in the mirror. That's when the voices start: *"Your thighs have more dimples than a Shirley Temple look-alike convention!"* they say, or *"What kind of eighties-wannabe haircut is that?"*

Then I take my older son to school and notice that the work-outside-the-home moms look all coiffed and stylish. The voices deride my writer's wardrobe of jeans and T-shirts.

At the grocery store with my youngest, I stand in front of the baby items and hear the little demons again: *"You should be making your own baby food—it's healthier."* In the household cleaners aisle, the stinkers hiss, *"When was the last time you dusted?"*

By the time I reach my house, I'm already defeated, and it's only 9:30 a.m.

I don't know who said it, but I believe it's true: Insecurity is the devil's playground. Or maybe the devil's *battleground* is a better word. His weapons attack from every side and usually leave a wound.

It's a constant war to not let the *"What kind of mother am I?"* questions run away with my emotions—and my peace.

Maybe you can relate. If my hunch is right, a lack of security is epidemic among moms. And let's face it: We have plenty to be concerned about. There are our figures, our finances, our future, and our families—just to name a few.

Recently, after making an impulse purchase at the check-out line, I noticed the headline on the women's magazine I had brought home: "Eat right, get fit, get organized, and *relax*."

Who are they kidding? I barely have time to take a shower each day, let alone have a perfect body or a spotless house. And relax while trying to keep it all together? Ha!

So I've decided to go on the offensive in this war on my thoughts and emotions. First, I'm going to stop letting the world's standards rule my mind. With God's help, I will tune more often into His Word—and less often into the TV. (And I'll trash the women's mags that spell out "25 Ways to Lose 25 Pounds in 25 Minutes"!)

Second, I'm going to try to quit comparing myself to other women. The truth is, they're probably as unsure about themselves as I am.

Third, when the prince of this world sends his darts toward me, I'll put up my shield of faith and ask myself: Just what is the *real* truth here?

The honest truth is: If my husband and I are raising our children by biblical standards, prayerfully doing the best we can, then God is pleased. As for my body, I know He wants me to be healthy and to take care of myself, but He couldn't care less what size my thighs are.

And you know what else? I'm betting that since Jesus was a carpenter, He doesn't mind a little dust.

NOTES FROM THE COACH

"You will be secure, because there is hope."

JOB 11:18 NIV

Don't copy the behavior and customs of this world,
but let God transform you into a new person
by changing the way you think.
Then you will know what God wants you to do,
and you will know how good and pleasing
and perfect his will really is.

ROMANS 12:2 NLT

In addition to all this,
take up the shield of faith,
with which you can extinguish
all the flaming arrows of the evil one.

EPHESIANS 6:16 NIV

Set your mind on the things above,
not on the things that are on earth.

COLOSSIANS 3:2 NASB

We use our powerful God-tools
for smashing warped philosophies,
tearing down barriers erected against
the truth of God,
fitting every loose thought
and emotion and impulse into
the structure of life shaped by Christ.

2 CORINTHIANS 10:5 MSG

Jesus and Jungle Gyms

(PART ONE)

*My work, my life,
must be in the spirit of a little child
seeking only to know the truth and follow it.*

GEORGE WASHINGTON CARVER

Sitting in a worship service one Sunday morning, I felt God nudging me to get involved with the church's preschool program.

As I pondered the myriad reasons I didn't want to take on that responsibility, it struck me that Jesus called His followers "little children." The Gospels portrayed Him as a man who loved kids and loved to teach. He even loved to *teach kids*. What a guy!

When *I* taught children, my back tightened, my eyes narrowed, and my head started to spin—kinda like Mr. Rogers meets *Mommy Dearest*. Not a pretty sight.

The funny thing is, I had always enjoyed teaching adults and teenagers. *Don't you have a place for me somewhere with them, Lord?* I asked. *They're clean, quiet, and interested in the lesson. Especially when I bring donuts.*

Then God gently reminded me that He had used my experiences with kids through the years to help me grow. I am more relaxed when I help at my son's school. I hug the kids, ask them questions, and listen to them. And I have a notebook handy for all the funny and amazing things they say.

Once, during a stint leading children's theater classes, I taught a six-year-old cutie with sparkly blue eyes and a mischievous grin. I never knew whether she was going to say something totally ridiculous or incredibly wise.

During one session, as I was auditioning the children for our year-end production, I noticed Ann pounding her head with a notebook.

"Ann!" I exclaimed. "What are you doing?"

"Hitting myself," she said.

"I can see that, but *why* are you doing it?"

"My finger hurts, and this makes me forget about it."

Another golden moment came when I volunteered to help with the four-year-olds at church, even though teaching Sunday school is sorta like being sent to Alcatraz—once you go in, you don't usually come out.

But as a minister's wife, I thought I would set a good example for the other adults and lead for a while. As it turns out, I nearly ruined my witness during my three-month tenure in the nursery.

Though the children were cute, they never listened. (I wasn't a parent at the time, or I wouldn't have taken it so personally.)

One Sunday, Katie interrupted the Bible story with something "very important" she needed to tell the class. I decided to let her speak, thinking she'd been overcome by a mature spiritual revelation—brought on by my excellent teaching, of course.

"What is it?" I asked.

"Happy birthday, Elvis!" she yelled.

I think that was my last Sunday.

I'll tell you the rest of the story tomorrow. . .for now, I have a strange compulsion to listen to "Love Me Tender."

Notes from the Coach

*"Beware that you don't look down upon
a single one of these little children.
For I tell you that in heaven their angels have
constant access to my Father."*

MATTHEW 18:10 TLB

*But Jesus said,
"Let the children come to me.
Don't stop them!
For the Kingdom of Heaven
belongs to such as these."*

MATTHEW 19:14 NLT

*At that time Jesus,
full of joy through the Holy Spirit, said,
"I praise you, Father, Lord of heaven and earth,
because you have hidden these things from the wise
and learned, and revealed them to little children."*

LUKE 10:21 NIV

*So you are all children of God
through faith in Christ Jesus.*

GALATIANS 3:26 NLT

Dear friends,
now we are children of God,
and what we will be
has not yet been made known.

1 JOHN 3:2 NIV

Jesus and Jungle Gyms

(PART TWO)

I talk in order to understand;
I teach in order to learn.

ROBERT FROST

As God and I discussed my previous teaching experiences, I brought up the fact that children could be difficult at times (as if this was news to Him!). *And by the way,* I thought, *so can teachers. One instructor in particular comes to mind.*

"Mrs. Morose" was that teacher. And between her and a curly slide, I was almost scarred for life.

To understand the importance of such a slide—the kind that starts way up high and twists and turns like a vertical roller coaster—you have to realize that I grew up in Dumas, Texas, where the most exciting event all year was the Lions Club members rolling up their sweetheart in meat-packing paper the night before the annual barbecue.

Anyhow, one day in third grade, I was selected by Mrs. Morose to go outside and check out a new addition to our playground. My instructions: Glance at the equipment without saying a word, come back in, and calmly report to the class.

But when I saw the new slide, I couldn't contain my joy. I jumped up and down, shouting, "A curly slide! A curly slide!"

Faster than the Lions Club could tenderize a beauty

queen, Mrs. Morose was at my side with ruler in hand. She grabbed my elbow and hissed, "I told you to be quiet! You'll be punished for this!"

And I was. I had to stay after school, writing something like "I will obey my teacher and not get excited over things kids are supposed to get excited about" on the blackboard one hundred times.

I'm not bitter, Lord, I thought. *Really, I'm not. But what if I end up like Mrs. Morose? I'd scar the kids for life!*

Then God pointed out that as hard as I try, I'm never going to be a perfect teacher. There is only *one* perfect teacher: Jesus.

A lot of people picture Jesus like Mrs. Morose—a stern instructor who carries around a sharp instrument, ready to "whap" you if you get out of line. In all honesty, I used to think of Him that way myself.

But I happen to know He's a lot of fun. In fact, the Gospels often show Jesus inviting the children to come to Him. Can't you see Him—like some cuddly, magnetic jungle gym—laughing as the moppets climb all over His back?

I think He would have loved a curly slide.

With those images flitting through my mind, I realized that Jesus' rapport with children didn't come from educational degrees or age-appropriate reading material. It came from His availability and obedience to God.

By the end of the service, my weeks of struggle with God had come to an end.

Okay, God, I thought, *I'll do it. I'll talk to the preschool minister and volunteer to help.*

And you know what? I've never regretted it.

NOTES FROM THE COACH

"Now go; I will help you speak
and will teach you what to say."

EXODUS 4:12 NIV

Let my teaching fall like rain
and my words descend like dew,
like showers on new grass,
like abundant rain on tender plants.

DEUTERONOMY 32:2 NIV

Come, my children,
listen as I teach you to respect the LORD.

PSALM 34:11 CEV

For you must teach others those things
you and many others have heard me speak about.
Teach these great truths to trustworthy men who will,
in turn, pass them on to others.

2 TIMOTHY 2:2 TLB

We preach Christ,
warning people not to add to the Message.
We teach in a spirit of profound common sense
so that we can bring each person to maturity.
To be mature is to be basic.
Christ! No more, no less.

COLOSSIANS 1:28 MSG

Sacred Storms

Storms make trees take deeper roots.

CLAUDE MCDONALD

Some young girls love dolls or horses. I was obsessed with storms.

Growing up, I lived in the Texas panhandle, where tornados were common.

Every year, from March to August, I kept vigil by watching the clouds and the weather portion of the news. Doppler radar came about during my childhood, and I watched with morbid fascination as the satellites tracked storm cells. The blood-red centers, surrounded by green and blue and yellow patches, blinked and crawled on my television set, ready to swallow anything in their path.

I'm sure my fears were heightened by my melancholy temperament, though I didn't know it at the time. But I recognized that a storm warning made my heart beat faster, and I knew all the county names in the Panhandle (and which direction they were from our ranch) by the time I was eight years old.

If I heard a *beep-beep-beep* during cartoons, I watched the screen for an update. If they didn't interrupt, I knew it wasn't a warning—just a "watch." If, however, the weatherman came on and announced a storm or tornado warning, I began to shiver with fear and anticipation.

But now that I'm grown, I'm still afraid of storms—just not the weather variety. I worry instead about financial storms, health tempests, relational winds, and job crises. My heart beats faster when I read about terror alerts or stock market fluctuations. And I shiver with fear when I hear about a carjacking in broad daylight.

So what's a storm-obsessed girl like me to do?

With God's help, I take a few practical steps to wrangle my fears. These three actions—as well as talking things out with my husband, friends, and the counselor I see periodically—keep my anxieties at reasonable levels:

First, I turn off the news. As my friend Wendy says, "If something big enough happens, I'll hear about it." They never report much good news, anyway—not the planes that don't crash, or the banks that weren't robbed, or the kids that weren't abducted.

Second, I try to meditate on scripture by writing Bible verses about hope and peace on index cards and taping them to my bathroom mirror.

Third, I pray. When I hear a siren or read an urgent e-mail, I immediately lift the need up in prayer. It helps me feel less immobilized and reminds me that God is ultimately in control of the world's weather.

Finally, I'm trying to see life's storms as what they are: opportunity for growth. (Don't you just hate that!) I can't control or predict the world's barometer, but I can run to God and let Him calm me. And that will lead to a closer relationship with the Weather Maker.

You know what? I think I'm getting better. Once in a while, I actually enjoy a real storm, with its wind, rain, thunder, and lightning.

As long as I'm safely inside.

NOTES FROM THE COACH

My heart is in anguish within me;
the terrors of death assail me.
Fear and trembling have beset me;
horror has overwhelmed me.
I said, "Oh, that I had the wings of a dove!
I would fly away and be at rest—
I would flee far away and stay in the desert;
I would hurry to my place of shelter,
far from the tempest and storm."

PSALM 55:4–8 NIV

For You have been a defense for the helpless,
A defense for the needy in his distress,
A refuge from the storm, a shade from the heat.

ISAIAH 25:4 NASB

When the storm is over, there's nothing left of the wicked;
good people, firm on their rock foundation, aren't even fazed.

PROVERBS 10:25 MSG

"Where is your faith?" he asked his disciples.
In fear and amazement they asked one another,
"Who is this? He commands even the winds
and the water, and they obey him."

LUKE 8:25 NIV

SECTION THREE

The First Lap

(Or Properly
Panicky and Desperate)

I want to have children, but my friends scare me.
One of my friends told me
she was in labor for thirty-six hours.
I don't even want to do anything
that feels good for thirty-six hours.

RITA RUDNER

When we brought our firstborn home from the hospital, I felt happy—and scared out of my mind. I was also still swollen with fluids, sore from a fresh incision *down there* (ouch!), and hormonal.

Like many newborns, Jordan slept during the day and cried all night. But when he didn't seem to be thriving, we visited the doctor and found out he wasn't nursing correctly. In fact, I didn't have enough milk because I was low on sleep and high on anxiety. For another week, I tried to nurse and/or pump. I finally gave up after finding out my blood pressure was sky-high.

Looking back, I realize I was a prime candidate for postpartum depression. I had already fought depression once, and though I had begun making strides while in counseling, I was not on medication. Combine the stress of new mommyhood with a fragile psyche and unrealistic expectations (I wanted to be a perfect parent) and you got me with PPD—Properly Panicky and Desperate.

About six weeks after Jordan was born, we visited my parents. After a short weekend at the ranch, I didn't want to come home. (That confused me—and it definitely scared Carey!) Soon after that, I had visions of driving off a bridge. I knew the idea was from Satan, and that I would never go through with it, but it frightened me just the same.

So I called my doctor and started on medication, which I've been on ever since. Carey and I went to a Christian counselor together for a while, and we made some lifestyle changes that helped me tremendously. God's grace—and the grace my counselor and family gave me—were both invaluable in my recovery.

However, for a long time, I felt guilty because I couldn't nurse Jordan. Some of that was legitimate pressure I felt from well-meaning friends and nurses, and some of it was just my being a perfectionist. I also felt ashamed that I was on medication for depression, thinking I should have been strong or "spiritual" enough to recover on my own.

I know better now.

Now I realize that God gives us each different temperaments and personalities, and we all have to make the best choices we can. In fact, one of my passions is to help women see that we're in this race *together*.

Let's not judge one another for the decisions we make about working or staying at home, nursing or bottle-feeding, cleaning or hiring help, and homeschooling versus public schooling.

Instead, I pray that we moms will give ourselves, and each other, grace—grace that Anne Lamott describes as "the force that infuses our lives and keeps letting us off the hook. . . . It's the help you receive when you have no bright ideas left, when you are empty and desperate and have discovered that your best thinking and most charming charm have failed you."

And, I might add, it's the grace that helps you forget childbirth and the early weeks so that—against all common sense—you decide to give your child a sibling.

NOTES FROM THE COACH

He tends his flock like a shepherd:
He gathers the lambs in his arms
and carries them close to his heart;
he gently leads those that have young.

ISAIAH 40:11 NIV

Save your people and bless your heritage.
Care for them; carry them like a good shepherd.

PSALM 28:9 MSG

"Judge not, that you be not judged."

MATTHEW 7:1 NKJV

By faith we have been made acceptable to God.
And now, because of our Lord Jesus Christ,
we live at peace with God.
Christ has also introduced us to God's
undeserved kindness on which we take our stand.
So we are happy,
as we look forward to sharing in the glory of God.
But that's not all! We gladly suffer,
because we know that suffering helps us to endure.
And endurance builds character,
which gives us a hope that will never disappoint us.
All of this happens because
God has given us the Holy Spirit,
who fills our hearts with his love.

ROMANS 5:1–5 CEV

A Pregnant Pause

If pregnancy were a book,
they would cut the last two chapters.

NORA EPHRON

As I write this, I'm seven months pregnant with our second child, and I have a confession: I don't like it! I feel like a penguin in bicycle shorts.

Several of my friends loved being pregnant. They didn't have morning sickness (I did—both times, for several months), or heartburn (ditto), or leg cramps (yup), or carpal tunnel syndrome (uh-huh).

I really despise those friends right now.

You know what's hardest about pregnancy? The waiting. They say it's nine months—but it's forty weeks, which to any person the least bit familiar with mathematics means *ten* months. Adding insult to injury, I found out the other day that a dog's gestation period is nine weeks. Weeks! Not fair.

I'm just an impatient person, anyway. I don't like waiting for bacon to fry—so I turn the heat up too far and scorch it. I don't like waiting for e-mail to download. I'm a big fan of drive-through dry cleaners, fast food, and instant credit.

Our culture has a fast-forward mentality. We love instant rice, one-hour photo developing, and twenty-four-hour grocery stores. If you want it right now, you can probably get it, depending on what "it" is.

However, if "it" is a satisfying job, an intimate relationship (with God, a mate, or a friend), a baby, a good prognosis, restored health, or financial stability—well, those things can't be rushed. And sometimes God's timing isn't always what we think best.

Have you heard of Saint Augustine? He wrote more than one thousand books and shaped Christian history. But before that, his mother, Monica, prayed for her wild and wayward son for forty years.

Biblical characters waited, too. Sarah, Hannah, and Elizabeth waited on a baby. Ruth waited on a husband. The Israelites waited on God's deliverance from Egypt. Paul waited on a thorn to be removed—and, as far as we know, it never was.

The apostle called "the Rock" wrote in 1 Peter 1:6–7 (NIV) that we should "greatly rejoice, though now for a little while you may have had to suffer grief in all kinds of trials. These have come so that your faith—of greater worth than gold, which perishes even though refined by fire—may be proved genuine and may result in praise, glory and honor when Jesus Christ is revealed."

My own times in God's waiting room have come pretty regularly. Like many of you, I've waited on a spouse, a child, healing for family members, salvation for friends, and more. Some of the prayers have been gloriously answered, far beyond what I could even imagine. Other times, God seems to have me in a holding pattern, as if He's pushed some cosmic "pause" button. Not fun. . .but obviously necessary for spiritual growth.

It occurs to me that maybe God is trying to teach me something with this whole pregnancy thing. And since it's definitely going to be my last one (I've already started trying to convince my husband that it's *his* turn to be in the hospital next!), maybe I'd better start learning.

And I will—as soon as I find some Tums.

NOTES FROM THE COACH

I wait in hope for your salvation, GOD.

GENESIS 49:18 MSG

In the morning, O LORD, you hear my voice;
in the morning I lay my requests
before you and wait in expectation.

PSALM 5:3 NIV

Wait patiently for the LORD. Be brave and courageous.
Yes, wait patiently for the LORD.

PSALM 27:14 NLT

At that time, people will say,
"The LORD has saved us! Let's celebrate.
We waited and hoped—now our God is here."

ISAIAH 25:9 CEV

I say to myself, "The LORD is my portion;
therefore I will wait for him."
The LORD is good to those whose hope is in him,
to the one who seeks him; it is good to wait quietly
for the salvation of the LORD.

LAMENTATIONS 3:24–26 NIV

Operation Enduring Sleep

*There never was a child so lovely
but his mother was glad to get him asleep.*

RALPH WALDO EMERSON

We call it Operation Enduring Sleep. My husband and I, the two-member coalition in this war on sleep deprivation, take our assignment very seriously. Our mission, should we decide to accept it, is to transfer our sleeping toddler, Jordan, from his car seat to his bed without waking him.

After we deploy ourselves, our first step is to unhook the buckle on his restraining device. Jordan sighs, and we freeze. Our lips purse, our foreheads crease, and we both wonder if we'll have to wave the white flag so early in the battle.

After unhooking our little soldier, we give silent instructions to one another. My husband Carey mouths, "You get him; I'll get the door." I nod in agreement.

Holding my breath, I slip Jordan's car seat strap over his head. So far, so good. Now the most dangerous part: the hoist. I carefully bring my son's heavy arms up over my shoulders, wrap one arm around his waist, and cover his head—so as not to bump it on the car door and accidentally end the operation.

My brave husband holds the door for me, and I walk past him. Trooper that he is, Carey has already been on a stealth mission in our son's bedroom. We both know that any miscalculation or stumble on my part would prove fatal to our plan, so Hubby has pulled the bedcovers back, darkened the room, and conducted a ground search for stray objects in Jordan's room.

As I reach the target, Jordan stirs a bit. I hesitate, re-calculate, and start humming a lullaby. Carey follows stealthily behind me, whispering encouragement. "Almost there," he says. "You can do it."

Then ever so gently, I place Jordan on his bed, take off his shoes, and cover his body with a blanket. I tiptoe away, giving Carey the thumbs-up sign. Mission accomplished.

But before we can be honorably discharged from our duties, we hear the one word that can bring an operation like this to its knees: "Mommy!"

Carey groans quietly. My heart starts to race. *No,* I think. *We've come too far to fail now! And I need a nap, too.* I decide to walk away slowly, ignore my child, and hope he's not really awake.

"Mommy!" Jordan cries, louder this time. I grimace at Carey. He shrugs, and I turn back around. Our son is sitting up in bed, rubbing his eyes. "I'm not tired now."

"You need more rest," I whisper. What I really mean, of course, is that *I* need more rest. In fact, I'm starting to wonder if sleep deprivation is fatal. "Go back to sleep."

Jordan hops off his bed, runs to my side, and raises his arms. "I want to hold you!" he says.

And so the mission is aborted. *Sneaky kid,* I think. He knows my weak spots, and he isn't afraid to exploit them.

As I take Jordan in my arms, I inhale his scent—a strange but comforting mixture of sweat, graham crackers, and baby soap. "Oh, well," I say to Carey. My hubby smiles and puts his arm around me, and we exit the nursery together, white flag waving.

Sometimes, losing the battle isn't such a bad deal.

NOTES FROM THE COACH

I lie down and sleep; I wake again,
*because the L*ORD *sustains me.*

PSALM 3:5 NIV

At day's end I'm ready for sound sleep,
*for you, G*OD*, have put my life back together.*

PSALM 4:8 MSG

Indeed, he who watches over Israel
will neither slumber nor sleep.

PSALM 121:4 NIV

It is useless for you to work so hard
from early morning until late at night,
anxiously working for food to eat;
for God gives rest to his loved ones.

PSALM 127:2 NLT

A Little Child Led Us

Children are unpredictable.
You never know what inconsistency
they're going to catch you in next.

FRANKLIN P. JONES

How do the little munchkins do it? Kids seem to have an extraordinary ability to sense when we're having a "serious discussion" with our spouse. They can say a few words and bring us to our knees—if not in prayer, then at least in shame.

Three years ago, Jordan—who was two and a half at the time—came into the room and interrupted a fight between Carey and me.

"Daddy, can I wear your wing?" he asked, pointing at Carey's left hand.

Carey stopped, looked at his son, and then at his wedding band, and said, "Okay, but stay right here."

My husband's eyes—which had flashed with anger moments before—now held questions.

"What does this wing mean, Daddy?" Jordan asked as he slipped it on his chubby finger.

Carey looked at me. "It means that Mommy and Daddy love each other very much and always will," he replied.

My tension-filled shoulders softened as I gazed at my child and my spouse. Jordan walked over to the corner of the room, turned around to us, and declared: "This wing means

I love Jesus. I want to give it to Him!"

I took in a sharp breath. Carey and I stared at Jordan, and then at each other. Then we laughed, and the tension in the room eased. How could we keep fighting after that reminder of our faith and our vows?

Another time, God used Jordan to help me nip a negative attitude in the bud.

I was zipping around the house, trying to complete a too-long list of chores before heading out the door. Along the way, I snapped at Jordan (who was then four).

Full of remorse, I sighed, sat down, and apologized to my son. "Jordan, honey," I said, "I'm really sorry I got angry at you. Mommy's just stressed out. Do you know what that means?"

He shook his head.

"It means I feel that I have too much to do and not enough time to do it. But that doesn't give me a reason to speak to you the way I did."

Jordan's forehead creased, and then he said, "But, Mommy, you're making God sad!"

Can you say "conviction"?

In *The Mystery of Children*, Mike Mason writes, "Children are meant to disrupt our lives and prick the bubble of our sinful pride. Who else is going to do this dirty work? Though a spouse will be happy to perform this service for us, children can sting us in a way that our peers cannot."

Amen to that.

And though I've never been a fan of chaos, as I get a little older (and hopefully a little wiser, too), I'm trying to let my kids be the holy disruption God wants them to be in my life.

Of course, I still get stressed. A lot. But when I do, I try to remember to slow down, say a prayer, and "breathe in, breathe out." That way I won't have to apologize—or listen to any more admonitions from my wiser-than-their-years little men.

Notes from the Coach

And a little child will lead them.

Isaiah 11:6 NIV

Nursing infants gurgle choruses about you;
toddlers shout the songs
That drown out enemy talk, and silence atheist babble.

Psalm 8:2 MSG

Wounds from a friend [or child!] can be trusted.

Proverbs 27:6 NIV

"I tell you the truth,
unless you change and become like little children,
you will never enter the kingdom of heaven."

Matthew 18:3 NIV

"Whoever welcomes this little child in my name welcomes me;
and whoever welcomes me welcomes the one who sent me.
For he who is least among you all—he is the greatest."

Luke 9:48 NIV

Out of the Mouths of Babes

*Parents learn a lot from their children
about coping with life.*

MURIEL SPARK

My friend Laurie has someone who keeps her on the straight and narrow. She loves this friend dearly, because she challenges Laurie to be the best she can be and yet still loves her unconditionally.

"However," says Laurie, "it's just plain hard to take good advice from a twelve-year-old.

"Yes," she says, "this all-knowing, Confucius-like friend is my fashion-conscious, eyeball-rolling daughter, Kailey."

I believe, and I'm sure you'll agree, that one of the reasons God put children on this earth was to keep their parents humble.

One of Laurie's episodes of "eating humble pie" at the feet of her daughter occurred when Kailey was eight. After many years of longing to visiting Glacier National Forest, their dream day had finally arrived. Laurie, her husband John, and Kailey had planned on camping and had heard that "Many Glacier Campground" offered the best views. But it also was known to sell out rather quickly.

Nonetheless, they decided to try and secure a campsite at

Many Glacier, on the opposite end of the park from the entrance, before it filled to capacity. After racing over mountain and stream, they arrived with only three campsites remaining. They quickly snatched one up.

Says Laurie, "When I wondered out loud what that cute little building was, located right smack in front of our campsite, my husband informed me that it was the RV dump site."

Laurie had *really* looked forward to a getting-back-to-God-and-nature vacation, but the existence of the dump site (which almost blocked their view of the mountains) threatened to overshadow her trip. She says, "I hate to admit it got to me. . .bad. I sulked around, grumbling about how we were finally in the beautiful park, and all we could see was a *dump* station!"

But then eight-year-old Kailey crawled up in her lap and said, "Mommy, look! You can *still* see the mountains from here!"

And as Laurie sat there pouting, God nudged her to think spiritually about her situation. She began to think, *How many other times have I let inconsequential, "dump station"-like problems get in my view of God's master plan?*

At first appearance, thought Laurie, *such circumstances can look huge, blocking out God's plan. But if I look beyond the ugly stuff, I can see the majesty in the distance.*

And so—once again—simple words from a child pulled a parent's eyes off herself and onto what was important.

One of God's richest blessings, and one of my favorite ironies, is that our children come into the world as people we're supposed to guide and direct, and then God uses them to form us—if we will only listen.

NOTES FROM THE COACH

Blessed is the man who finds wisdom,
the man who gains understanding.

PROVERBS 3:13 NIV

When pride comes, then comes dishonor,
But with the humble is wisdom.

PROVERBS 11:2 NASB

But God chose the foolish things
of the world to shame the wise;
God chose the weak things
of the world to shame the strong.
He chose the lowly things of this world
and the despised things—
and the things that are not—
to nullify the things that are,
so that no one may boast before him.
It is because of him that you are in Christ Jesus,
who has become for us wisdom from God—
that is, our righteousness, holiness and redemption.
Therefore, as it is written:
"Let him who boasts boast in the Lord."

1 CORINTHIANS 1:27–31 NIV

SECTION FOUR

Using Proper Equipment

The Solace of Solitude

*I never found the companion that
was so companionable as solitude.*

HENRY DAVID THOREAU

Some days, I just don't feel super-spiritual, despite a call to ministry, a wonderful Christian family, a great church, some seminary training, and a God who has been super-faithful.

On those days, I long for the solace of solitude—perhaps a bubble bath, complete with candles, soft music, and a fresh glass of raspberry tea. However, I'm more likely to get five rushed minutes (if I'm lucky) in the shower without my sons setting the cat on fire.

And other women around me have equally challenging, if different, schedules:

Ruth is the mother of two kiddos in diapers. She longs for telemarketers to call, just so she can have adult conversation. And though she'd love to listen to an entire CD by Norah Jones, the song that gets played most often around her house is "The Wheels on the Bus." Time alone? Ha!

Anna is a single mom who works as a secretary and a part-time piano instructor. Her days are filled shuttling her two teenagers to/from school and activities, working, and home maintenance. Time to call her own? Not likely.

Ruth, Anna, and I find it almost impossible to carve out time for ourselves. And yet, whether we realize it or not, we each need solitude. (Some personality types—extroverts in particular—don't seem to crave it as much as others. But even outgoing women can find serenity, hope, and a renewed sense of creativity after being alone.)

Why? Solitude replenishes and refreshes us. It's a necessary, and often overlooked, facet of a grace-full life. My friends and I laugh about it, but it's sad: None of us make time to be alone anymore. We're too busy driving our kids to soccer practice, working outside the home, and helping with church activities. There's simply no time for recreation or rest. And what's even sadder—we often feel like we're irreplaceable and indestructible.

I've decided I don't want to postpone balance or rest any longer. I know what it does to my body and soul when I do.

Ladies, I've begun to realize that *only cats have nine lives*. We have but one. And it is a super-myth that you can be a superwoman. In fact, you can do some of it, and have some of it done, but if you try to do it all, you'll be done in.

And since you are only one person, take care of yourself! Maybe that will mean scheduling a sitter so you can have some time alone. Perhaps you can trade child care with a friend for a couple of hours a week—delicious hours in which you do something for yourself, and not for your kids or hubby. Or maybe you'll decide to take up a new hobby and have your husband take over tending the home fires one night a week. Only you can decide what kind of solitude you need to replenish your mind and soul.

I like what Pearl S. Buck once said: "I love people. I love my family, my children. . .but inside myself is a place where I live all alone and that's where you renew your springs that never dry up."

So my challenge to you is to say no to some less-important things once in a while, so that you can say yes to yourself.

Periodically, let God fill your empty reservoir in the solace of solitude.

I think you'll be super-glad you did.

NOTES FROM THE COACH

After He had sent the crowds away,
He went up on the mountain by Himself to pray;
and when it was evening,
He was there alone.

MATTHEW 14:23 NASB

He lets me rest in green meadows;
he leads me beside peaceful streams.

PSALM 23:2 NLT

"The Lord will fight for you;
you need only to be still."

EXODUS 14:14 NIV

When you pray,
go into a room alone and close the door.
Pray to your Father in private.

He knows what is done in private,
and he will reward you.

Matthew 6:6 cev

So He Himself often withdrew
into the wilderness and prayed.

Luke 5:16 nkjv

The Hardest Job You'll Ever Love

*Not only is a woman's work never done,
the definition keeps changing.*

BILL COPELAND

In my thirty-plus years, I've had some interesting jobs: legal secretary, cowhand, missionary, youth minister, news writer, and—believe it or not—telemarketer for a roofing firm. (That last job lasted about a week, because my stomach was constantly in knots.)

But by far, the hardest job I've ever had is motherhood. I know you'll agree that being a mom ranks right up there with sewer installers, kindergarten teachers, and soldiers as the toughest, least-heralded of all professions.

In fact, I think we moms should take the U.S. Army slogan, "The hardest job you'll ever love" and make it ours. That sums up motherhood pretty well.

The other day, I was using a spa gift certificate my darling hubby had given me for Christmas (sorry, girls, he's taken), and it occurred to me that our society is all messed up about careers. Here I was, at a place where technicians were getting a dollar *a minute* for rubbing my body with fragrant oils and painting my toenails, and my son was being taught to read at the public school by a woman making pennies.

It got me thinking. . .what if we paid people what they were worth to us *moms*?

We'd place teachers—who help guide our children toward a brighter future and give us great ideas about how to control our kids at home—on the top of the money totem pole. If we gave them a dollar a minute, like the beauty-treatment folks, they'd make about $100,000 a year, before taxes. That's more like it!

How about the nurse and receptionist at the pediatrician's office? They're the ones who spend most of the time with our kiddos when they're sick. Let's hike their salaries up to (at least) spa-tech level.

Pastors should get a raise, too. They provide a sounding board for our questions and guide us in God's truth. And they negotiate with church committees for good nursery workers. If we paid them at a dollar a minute—assuming the average pastor works fifty hours a week (which is probably on the low side)—we'd be providing ministers with over $140,000 a year.

And what about moms? If we got paid what we're worth, no one could afford us. Right, ladies? Since we work 24/7, 365 days a year, our salary—at beauty-technician levels—would be $525,600.

Okay—that's not going to happen. But I don't think many of us will be turning in our resignation any time soon.

After all, we can also look at our job as the best-paid one in the world—because we get compensated in ways that other people don't.

Just last week from my son, I got a bouquet of cattails, a science fair trophy, three "I missed you's," and lots of sloppy kisses.

Would I trade that for stock options, a penthouse office suite, or a lifetime of spa treatments?

Not in a million years.

NOTES FROM THE COACH

Hard work means prosperity;
only fools idle away their time.

PROVERBS 12:11 NLT

Hard work always pays off;
mere talk puts no bread on the table.

PROVERBS 14:23 MSG

My heart took delight in all my work,
and this was the reward for all my labor.

ECCLESIASTES 2:10 NIV

Therefore, my dear brothers, stand firm.
Let nothing move you.
Always give yourselves fully to the work of the Lord,
because you know that your labor in the Lord is not in vain.

1 CORINTHIANS 15:58 NIV

And she always works hard.

PROVERBS 31:17 CEV

Law and Disorder

*Oh, what a tangled web do parents weave
when they think their children are naive.*

OGDEN NASH

One day when my son Jordan was four, just as I was pondering the challenges of parenting in the new millennium, he deliberately disobeyed me. Frustrated, I grabbed him, placed him on my knee, and raised my hand to give him a swat. Suddenly, he looked up at me and said, "I smell a lawsuit!"

Okay, I thought, *political correctness has just gone way too far.*

Actually, he never said that. But if he had, maybe he wouldn't have been too far off using legalese in a discipline debate. In fact, after thinking it through, I realized that frazzled moms frequently use law terms—or, at least, strategies of law—in parenting. (Finally, all those hours spent viewing *Law and Order* are paying off!)

Here are a few examples that we "legal-eagle moms" often employ:

Opening arguments—"Wouldn't it be fun to clean up
   your room?" we kindly ask our charges. "Let's make it
   into a game—with candy prizes."
Discovery—"What is that green thing under your bed—
   and *why are you eating it?*"

Objection—"Don't you use that tone of voice with me, young woman!"

See you in chambers—"If you'll stay on the commode for five minutes, I'll sit in the bathroom with you and read *Once Upon a Potty*. Again."

Plead the Fifth—"Because God made it that way." (This all-purpose answer works surprisingly well in a variety of situations, at least until the kid reaches kindergarten.)

Cross-examination—"Where did you get that tattoo?" and "Who will be at the party?" for teens; "Why are you licking the carpet?" and "Where's the gerbil?" for younger tykes.

Leading the witness—"Don't you want a delicious green bean?" we ask our little loves, who have ingested exactly four bites of veggies in their lives (sorry—French fries don't count!). My hubby—who cooks veggies in bacon grease just to get our son to taste them—sometimes adds, "They have *good flavor* on them."

Motion to suppress—The lightning-fast hand movement we make to cover our wee one's mouth when we're out in public and he/she yells, "Mommy, why is that lady so fat?"

Negotiating a settlement—"If you are really good in the store, I'll buy you a kids' meal from Burger King on the way home."

Plea bargaining—"If you go to bed right now, without fussing, you can play with sharp things all day tomorrow."

And, finally, we come to the end of our struggle. It's ten o'clock, they've worn us down, and we decide to use the mother of all defenses:

Closing arguments—"Because I said so. And I'm the grown-up. Nyah-nyah-nyah-nyah."

I'm sure glad God isn't as petty as I am in His parental dealings with this disobedient child. When I try His patience, He is always fair, doling out just the right balance of justice and mercy. He never, ever says, "Nyah-nyah-nyah-nyah."

And He doesn't even make me eat green beans.

I'll take Him as my legal counsel any day.

NOTES FROM THE COACH

*"Teach them the decrees and laws,
and show them the way to live and the duties
they are to perform."*

EXODUS 18:20 NIV

*"There must be Someone in heaven
who knows the truth about me,
in highest heaven,
some Attorney who can clear my name."*

JOB 16:19 MSG

*Generous in love—
God, give grace! Huge in mercy—
wipe out my bad record.*

PSALM 51:1 MSG

When justice is done,
it brings joy to the righteous but terror to evildoers.

PROVERBS 21:15 NIV

Yet the LORD longs to be gracious to you;
he rises to show you compassion.
For the LORD is a God of justice.
Blessed are all who wait for him!

ISAIAH 30:18 NIV

My Prayer— Ahem, Water—Closet

*Some people think that God is in the details,
but I have come to
believe that God is in the bathroom.*

ANNE LAMOTT

If you're like me, you constantly feel guilty about not praying or reading the Bible enough—if at all. But when the dishwasher breaks, my hormones are raging, a work deadline is looming, and the kids are whining, sometimes I just want to scream. And fit in a daily quiet time? You've got to be kidding me!

That's why Susanna Wesley, one of the mothers of the Methodist church, is one of my role models. In addition to being an Anglican minister's wife, Susanna managed a full-to-the-brim household, homeschooled her children (even writing some of their textbooks), and studied theology. When her husband was away, she filled his pulpit. Eventually her fifteenth child, John, and her seventeenth, Charles, founded the Methodist church.

Whew. The overview of her life makes me tired just writing it! Yet Susanna's most admirable trait? She was never too busy for spiritual nourishment.

John Wesley once recorded that his mother never let *anything* interfere with her times with God. Often, she would put her apron over to head to signal that she was not to be disturbed during prayer time.

I don't have an apron. (As one writer friend of mine says, "My apron burned in the fire.") But I did come up with a way to be alone and pray, even during the raising-toddler years.

As a busy mom who needed and wanted to pray, I was looking for ways to find peace in my prayer life, instead of always feeling guilty. I was also tired of being scatterbrained—I could rarely remember whom or what I had promised to pray for.

So one day when I had a few hours by myself, I wrote down every need (for myself, family, friends, church, community, nation, and world) I could think of. Then I divided them into thirty-one equal segments and put them in a notebook.

I have this notebook—believe it or not—in the bathroom, where I do have a few precious minutes alone each day. (This also fulfills Jesus' command to "go into your closet and pray," though I'm not sure He actually meant a water closet!)

In my closet, I speak to God about the items that correspond to the day of the month. That way, I can pray over the multitude of needs in my life—one day and one minute at a time.

If "water closet praying" isn't for you, here are some different ideas about fitting prayer into a kid-full life:

Pray as you work out.

Light a candle when someone dear to you has a need. Every time you see the flame, lift her or his request up to God.

Pray while driving/commuting.

Pray while waiting on kids at sports practices.

Sign up for prayer lists online, and pray as you read the e-mail messages.

And remember, no matter how or when we choose to pray, God is pleased when we make the effort. He just wants to hear from us—even if our calls come from the bathroom!

Notes from the Coach

"May you hear the humble and earnest requests
from me and your people Israel when
we pray toward this place.
Yes, hear us from heaven where you live,
and when you hear, forgive."

2 Chronicles 6:21 nlt

I call on you, O God,
for you will answer me;
give ear to me and hear my prayer.

Psalm 17:6 niv

"You'll pray to him and he'll listen;
he'll help you do what you've promised."

Job 22:27 msg

On the day I called, You answered me;
You made me bold with strength in my soul.

Psalm 138:3 nasb

*Oh, don't be so angry with us, L*ORD*.*
Please don't remember our sins forever.
Look at us, we pray,
and see that we are all your people.

ISAIAH 64:9 NLT

Journaling for the Soul

Writing is the axe that breaks the frozen sea within.

FRANZ KAFKA

We moms don't have much privacy. (Is that the understatement of the year, or what?) Maybe that's why I am such a fan of journaling—periodically keeping a private record of whatever is sacred, scary, and/or special.

Does the thought of writing something—anything—make your shoulders tense up? Maybe journaling seems like one more burden to cram into your already-packed schedule. It doesn't have to be that way.

Regularly recording your thoughts, feelings, dreams, and goals can be beneficial to your body, mind, and spirit. In fact, instead of adding to the pressures I face as a working mom, journaling actually helps keep me from going crazy.

I've never kept a diary—that smacks of duty and dailyness to me. But since I was eleven, I've journaled. In dozens of blank books, I've jotted down prayers, thoughts, poems, scriptures, lists, and inspiring quotes.

One major benefit of journaling is that you have a record of your life. I've got a shelf full of books filled with high school angst, college worries, and newlywed frustrations. My husband especially likes to look back at my "crush of the week" journals from junior high. They provide hours of free entertainment!

Here's a sample entry from eighth grade:

Boys Who Like Me: 1) Justin 2) Bill 3) Brian
Boys Who I Like: 1) James 2) Casey 3) Trent

Notice none of the names are the same!

As an adult, I've stopped keeping lists of cute boys. But I sometimes list my goals, which has helped me to define them more clearly and plan little steps to reaching them. Other days, I scratch down ideas or "to do's," which clears my mind and leaves me feeling peaceful instead of panicked. And always, I try to be gut-level honest with the paper, allowing long-hidden emotions to surface—a healing process I highly recommend.

Often, the Holy Spirit brings scriptures to mind while journaling, and I'll look them up and record them as encouragement during a trial. And frequently, the simple act of writing my problems down has opened up solutions I'd never considered before.

Every time I take a few moments to "break the frozen sea within," I feel lighter and less cluttered.

Not convinced about journaling's merits? Try scheduling a writing session one day a week, and write your prayers and concerns about the things that make you sad or frightened. Or record the answered prayers or blessings God has graced you with. I'll bet that you feel less scattered after jotting your thoughts down on paper. You might even feel those shoulders loosening up.

In her book *Fresh-Brewed Life*, journaling advocate and actress Nicole Johnson writes, "A journal is a tool, a flower, a canvas, a safety deposit box, a cup of coffee with a friend. It can hold your dreams, record your life, challenge your thinking, refresh your soul, tickle your sides, and redirect your steps."

Go ahead, try it! You might just find that journaling is, indeed, good for your soul.

NOTES FROM THE COACH

Then the LORD said to Moses,
"Write down these words,
for in accordance with these words
I have made a covenant with you and with Israel."

EXODUS 34:27 NIV

This is the Message Jeremiah received from GOD....
"Write everything I tell you in a book."

JEREMIAH 30:1-2 MSG

Then the LORD replied:
"Write down the revelation and make it plain."

HABAKKUK 2:2 NIV

Having carefully investigated
all of these accounts from the beginning,
I have decided to write a careful summary for you,
to reassure you of the truth of all you were taught.

LUKE 1:3-4 NLT

*"Therefore write the things which you have seen,
and the things which are,
and the things which will take place after these things."*

REVELATION 1:19 NASB

SECTION FIVE

Hopping Over the Hurdles

Confessions of a Chocoholic

*Probably nothing in the world arouses more hope
than the first four hours of a diet.*

DAN BENNETT

I love to eat; I always have. Chocolate? Yum. Salsa and cheese dip? Love 'em! Italian food? Gimme some!

When I was younger, my body accepted my sometimes-poor eating habits with no adverse side effects. But as I stopped growing in height, I started growing in girth. In fact, each time my life changed in a dramatic way, I put on weight.

First, there was the freshman fifteen. Then I put on the newlywed twenty, and later, the new baby thirty. By that time—my late twenties—I realized something had to change. So I began to diet.

And believe me, I tried them all. But Slim-Fast made me gag, a low-carb diet made me crazy, and Weight Watchers made me hungry. I even tried a plan that had its followers ingesting one kind of food all day, and then switching. For example, one day was grapes, the next pineapple—and I hate pineapple! It was supposed to burn fat, but it just burned me out.

The South Beach diet was working well for me until I got pregnant and had to stop doing it. (Now I'm thinking about creating a "Nude Beach Diet." You observe—fully clothed, of course, a nude beach. Then you either feel great about your body and don't *want* to diet anymore, or you have the motivation to never eat again. Could be quite popular, don't you think?)

But I finally came to the conclusion that unless I wanted to look like a Macy's Day parade balloon by the time I was forty, I had to make a lifestyle change. That meant I was going to have to alter my habits and let God give me some discipline (uh-oh!). God also challenged me to start looking to Him to meet some of the needs I was filling through unhealthy eating patterns.

So I started to exercise regularly and began to choose smaller portions and healthy alternatives at stores and restaurants. And you know what? It worked. I'm still not model-thin, by any means. I never will be, and most days, I'm okay with that. But I feel much better—physically and spiritually.

Throughout my struggle with weight, God has reminded me time and again that *He* wants to be my food. Some days I let Him fill me up with His peace and power, and other days I run (again!) to the candy machine.

I've learned that my spiritual life is a lot like my eating habits. It's a daily battle to let Jesus, the Bread of Life, be my sustenance. It's much easier to run to the television, read a gossip magazine, or call a friend than it is to take the time to tell God what's bothering me and let Him work on my problems.

So my earnest prayer has become, "Lord Jesus, help me to hunger for You more than I hunger for earthly food. Make me as excited about spending time with You as I am about going out to eat."

And sometimes I add this postscript: "One more thing, Lord—please let there be chocolate in heaven."

Notes from the Coach

"Life is more than food, and the body more than clothes."

LUKE 12:23 NIV

In the meantime, the disciples pressed him,
"Rabbi, eat. Aren't you going to eat?"
He told them, "I have food to eat you know nothing about."
The disciples were puzzled.
"Who could have brought him food?"
Jesus said, "The food that keeps me going is that I do the
will of the One who sent me, finishing the work he started."

JOHN 4:31-34 MSG

Jesus answered, "It is written:
'Man does not live on bread alone,
but on every word that comes from the mouth of God.' "

MATTHEW 4:4 NIV

Then Jesus said to them, "Most assuredly,
I say to you, Moses did not give you the bread from heaven,
but My Father gives you the true bread from heaven.
For the bread of God is He who comes down from
heaven and gives life to the world."
Then they said to Him, "Lord, give us this bread always."

And Jesus said to them,
"I am the bread of life.
He who comes to Me shall never hunger,
and he who believes in Me shall never thirst."

JOHN 6:32–35 NKJV

Going for the Gold

*Parenthood remains the greatest
single preserve of the amateur.*

ALVIN TOFFLER

I come from a very competitive family. We're not super-outdoorsy or athletic, but just try to come between one of us and a piece of fried chicken! At our annual family reunion, we have horseshoe and Ping-Pong tournaments for kids and adults, complete with poster-board tracking systems and trophies.

So I got to thinking: If this parenting thing were an Olympic sport, perhaps I could be a medalist—or at least a contender. See if you can identify with some of these sports my friends and I practice:

Weight lifting—Sure, those big guys in spandex can bench-press twice their body weight, but can they carry a thirty-pound toddler, a purse full of the latest Happy Meal toys, and a bag of half-melted groceries?

High jump—My buddies have hit the ceiling so many times after their teenagers came home an hour past curfew that they've started wearing bicycle helmets while waiting on the sofa.

Long jump—There may not be a regulation long-jump course in my living room, but I can cover the distance from the couch to the television in less than a second in order to shield my son's eyes from a suggestive commercial.

Curling—This event doesn't involve a broom and a funny-looking puck, but it does require you to raise your upper lip at the gross dinner conversation your teenage son is having with his father. Extra points are awarded for not making gagging sounds.

Hurdles—Any parent is a pro at this. It comes from years of experience going to the bathroom in the middle of the night without stepping on clothes, backpacks, or small living creatures.

Balance beam—I may not be able to do a backflip on a four-inch piece of wood, but I'd like to see any Olympian juggle kids' practices, church obligations, work, marriage, and family demands without getting dizzy and taking a dive.

While parenting is not actually a competitive sport, we moms are champions at comparing ourselves to others and measuring our kids against impossible standards. We want our children to be as fast as Michael Johnson, as funny as Scott Hamilton, and as good-looking as Bart Conner. Unfortunately, that usually doesn't happen—and we feel like the competitor who just missed the bronze medal.

Before I became a mom, I read all the "right" parenting books, attended classes, and decided that I would never spank, yell, criticize, or use television as a babysitter. I thought I was being realistic! After all, I didn't say that I would nurse for two years, use cloth diapers, or sew my son's clothing out of recycled draperies.

There's nothing wrong with wanting the best for my family. But I need to remember that I'm human, and my

children are, too. I'm the queen of unrealistic expectations—
I have the crown and scepter in my closet to prove it—which
only sets me up for disappointment.

So I'm slowly learning, by the merciful grace of God, to
let go of my unattainable goals and simply enjoy the sons He
has given me. After all, God's the only perfect parent. And
He's written the only parenting manual that really matters:
the Holy Bible.

NOTES FROM THE COACH

*Therefore, since we are surrounded by
such a great cloud of witnesses,
let us throw off everything that hinders
and the sin that so easily entangles,
and let us run with perseverance
the race marked out for us.
Let us fix our eyes on Jesus,
the author and perfecter of our faith,
who for the joy set before him endured the cross,
scorning its shame,
and sat down at the right hand of the throne of God.
Consider him who endured such opposition
from sinful men,
so that you will not grow weary and lose heart.*

HEBREWS 12:1–3 NIV

I'm not saying that I have this all together,
that I have it made.
But I am well on my way,
reaching out for Christ,
who has so wondrously reached out for me.

PHILIPPIANS 3:12 MSG

Have you lost your senses?
After starting your Christian lives in the Spirit,
why are you now trying to become
perfect by your own human effort?

GALATIANS 3:3 NLT

It does not, therefore,
depend on man's desire or effort,
but on God's mercy.

ROMANS 9:16 NIV

Falling into Grace

The pursuit of perfection often impedes improvement.

GEORGE F. WILL

I love autumn, with its crisp leaves, brisk air, and changing colors. However, as a recovering perfectionist, I've had many autumns in the past that fell short of my "ideal" fall. Here are my usual expectations, followed by a dose of reality:

1. My husband will lovingly help me pick out just the right pumpkin for our son's kindergarten craft project.
   Reality: Carey is so swamped with work that I run to Wal-Mart on October 30 and get a leftover shaped like a Hobbit.
2. The Christian child I'm raising will help me shop for Thanksgiving baskets for needy families.
   Reality: Five-year-old Jordan stays in the toy aisle during the entire excursion, whining that he *needs* a "Home for the Holidays" G.I. Joe.
3. I'll make pumpkin cookie platters for all the neighbors, with an evangelical tract attached.
   Reality: Only when I see the neighbors packing to leave for the Thanksgiving holidays do I begin to bake, and then realize I need to borrow half the ingredients from those same neighbors.
4. The extended family will all be together—healthy

and happy—for a quiet, reflective Thanksgiving.

Reality: Two siblings don't even show up, the "crazy uncle" shows everybody his newest surgical scar, and my giblet gravy looks more like— well, let's not even go there.

This year was no different. Since Carey had to work on Halloween, I took Jordan to our church's fall festival. It was a doozy—bounce houses, pony rides, Bible-themed carnival games, costume contests, and an inflatable obstacle course. I expected a fun-filled night, complete with many Kodak moments.

However, only an hour into our evening, Jordan came off the big slide in tears. My first thought was that someone had picked on him. My second thought was finding the little bully and—well, we were in the church parking lot, so I decided against physical violence.

"What's wrong, sweetie?" I asked.

He wouldn't tell me, but I soon figured out that he had torn his pants. And no amount of cajoling would get him back in the game.

So we went home and watched *America's Funniest Home Videos.*

I was a little distraught at how our evening had turned out, especially when the doorbell rang. Since we hadn't planned on being home, I didn't have enough candy for trick-or-treaters.

"Mom, kids are at the door!" Jordan yelled at me as I frantically looked for granola bars or fruit.

"I don't have enough candy," I lamented as he kept pointing to the door.

"They can have mine," Jordan said as he reached into his purple pumpkin, full of prizes from carnival games. With my mouth agape, I opened the door and watched him gleefully fill the trick-or-treaters' sacks.

The rest of the evening, my son had a ball passing out his hard-won candy to strangers with painted faces, and I marveled at the child who had reminded me: Life may tear your expectations to pieces once in a while, but focusing on others helps you forget your troubles.

And being a perfectionist isn't near as much fun as it's made out to be.

NOTES FROM THE COACH

"Take my yoke upon you and learn from me,
for I am gentle and humble in heart,
and you will find rest for your souls."

MATTHEW 11:29 NIV

"This core holy people will not do wrong.
They won't lie, won't use words to flatter or seduce.
Content with who they are and where they are,
unanxious, they'll live at peace."

ZEPHANIAH 3:13 MSG

"You're blessed when you're content with
just who you are—no more, no less.

That's the moment you find yourselves proud owners
of everything that can't be bought."

MATTHEW 5:5 MSG

I am not saying this because I am in need,
for I have learned to be content
whatever the circumstances.
I know what it is to be in need,
and I know what it is to have plenty.
I have learned the secret of being content
in any and every situation,
whether well fed or hungry,
whether living in plenty or in want.

PHILIPPIANS 4:11–12 NIV

Is the Proverbs 31 Woman for Real?

*I tried to do so many things for God
that I missed being with God.
But I've learned—the hard way—
life isn't about keeping it all together.
It's about trusting the One who can.*

NICOLE JOHNSON

Do you ever feel intimidated by the Proverbs 31 woman—the one who sewed like Betsy Ross, volunteered like Mother Teresa, and ran her own business like Oprah? I know I have.

But I have a theory about that "perfect" biblical woman. As we know, Solomon wrote Proverbs, and Solomon had hundreds of wives. So, dear reader, I believe the Proverbs 31 woman was a *composite*. Solomon simply took the best qualities from several wives and created a word portrait of his "ideal" companion. (It works for me!)

Seriously, I've often felt discouraged while reading that famous biblical chapter. I can't tell the difference between soufflé and flambé, and—to my mother's horror—I can't even sew on a button. I've ruined laundry, sent "belated birthday" cards, and taken my kid to preschool in my pajamas more times than I can count.

For years, every time I read Proverbs 31, I felt as if this

spiritual superwoman was up in heaven, mocking my paltry attempts at being a wife, friend, mom, and daughter. I didn't realize that the chapter was most likely an overview of the woman's entire life (and not one day, week, or even month)—or that, as my friend and fellow author Char Barnes says, "In Proverbs 31, the woman's children rise up and call her blessed. Toddlers don't rise up and bless their mother—this lady obviously had grown children."

After I began to experience panic attacks because of my perfectionism, I realized God was calling me to a different standard than the one I had erroneously set for myself. And through the wisdom of a godly counselor, I discovered that in the verse I had taken as my mantra—"Be perfect, therefore, as your heavenly Father is perfect" (Matthew 5:48 NIV)—the word "perfect" can also be translated as "mature."

Part of my becoming mature has meant learning that I have limits. We have just one life, and our Savior died and rose again so that it could be an abundant life. When Jesus said in John 10:10 (NIV), "I have come that they may have life, and have it to the full," He wasn't talking about a day planner jam-packed with activities or a schedule crammed with "to do's."

Christ was speaking about a life of purpose, contentment, and peace. As a busy wife and mom, I've come to believe that we can experience abundant life daily *if* we get off the hamster wheel of perfectionism, recognize our limits, and nestle close to Jesus.

When I remember that He loved me enough to leave the perfection of heaven and soil His feet with the crud of earth, I can see myself as He does. I can accept God's mercy and impart that mercy to the imperfect people around me.

Then—and only then—can I live each day with joy and *perfect* peace.

Notes from the Coach

A wife of noble character who can find?
She is worth far more than rubies.
Her husband has full confidence in her
and lacks nothing of value.
She brings him good, not harm,
all the days of her life....
She is clothed with strength and dignity;
she can laugh at the days to come.
She speaks with wisdom,
and faithful instruction is on her tongue....
Charm is deceptive, and beauty is fleeting;
but a woman who fears the LORD is to be praised.

PROVERBS 31:10–12, 25–26, 30 NIV

"Walk with me and work with me—watch how I do it.
Learn the unforced rhythms of grace.
I won't lay anything heavy or ill-fitting on you.
Keep company with me and you'll learn to
live freely and lightly."

MATTHEW 11:29–30 MSG

It's Good to Be Queen

*Boys are beyond the range of
anybody's sure understanding,
at least when they are between the ages of
eighteen months and ninety years.*

JAMES THURBER

Can I make an "I feel like a horrible mother saying this" confession? During the fifth month of my second—and hopefully last—pregnancy, when I found out I was carrying a boy instead of a girl, I was sorely disappointed. The girlie side of me wanted to have someone to dress up in lace and ribbons, give tea parties, play dolls, and "shop till you drop" with.

The other side of me was relieved. I mean, I do know how to raise boys. . .sort of.

Jordan was with Carey and me at the time of the ultra-important ultrasound. He was thrilled! "Mommy, now you have three boys to take care of!" he crowed.

"No, honey," I replied. "You'll have to all take care of me!"

But as I began to rifle through my oldest son's baby clothes in preparation for our new arrival, my heart softened. The clothes were adorable—and they reminded me of how cute and sweet little boys are. Then my son asked to watch videos of himself when he was a toddler, and my heart melted some more. And I actually started getting excited about this boy thing. . . .

After all, I know that as a mom of two boys:

I'll wipe away tears of laughter as they say things like, "Mom! Look how I can pick my nose with my big toe!" while demonstrating.

I'll wipe away tears of joy when they tell me, "Mom, I love you so much—I'll never let anything happen to you."

I'll enjoy lots of dandelion bouquets and homemade cards.

I'll be the love of my sons' lives, at least until they discover girls.

I won't have to keep the house too clean, because they won't care.

I don't have to worry about cooking elaborate meals. Give 'em a hot dog baked in a crescent roll, and they're in heaven.

Once they're potty trained, I won't have to take them to the bathroom in restaurants—too bad for my hubby.

My friend Heather (mom to two boys) e-mailed me a few more benefits of having an all-testosterone household:

You never feel obligated to pay for a wedding.

Clothes are not an issue. Most boys are happy with jeans and a T-shirt.

Most of us moms have enough hormones and emotions for the entire family!

When Dad takes the boys for a "boy only" outing, it means relaxing time for Mom. Ahhh!

With the help of friends like Heather, I'm trying (and mostly succeeding) to trust that God has given me exactly what I need. When this baby arrives, he will be just the infant God ordained for our family. And, wonder of wonders, I will be the mom ordained for him.

You know, as I feel this child's prenatal kicks and hiccups, I'm already starting to relax and love him. And I know the moment I see him, I'll think he's perfect, in every sense of the word.

Like Heather says, "It is good to be Queen."

Notes from the Coach

*Sons are a heritage from the L*ORD,
children a reward from him.
Like arrows in the hands of a warrior
are sons born in one's youth.

PSALM 127:3–4 NIV

But Mary kept all these things,
and pondered them in her heart.

LUKE 2:19 KJV

"You parents—if your children ask for a loaf of bread,
do you give them a stone instead?
Or if they ask for a fish, do you give them a snake?
Of course not! If you sinful people know
how to give good gifts to your children,
how much more will your heavenly Father
give good gifts to those who ask him."

MATTHEW 7:9–11 NLT

Every good and perfect gift is from above,
coming down from the Father of the heavenly lights,
who does not change like shifting shadows.

JAMES 1:17 NIV

SECTION SIX

Handing It Off

The Red Sea Place

Have you come to the Red Sea place in your life where,
in spite of all you can do, there is no way out,
there is no way back, there is no other way but through?

ANNIE JOHNSON FLINT

If you're like me, you probably feel "stuck" sometimes. Every day, I look toward the top of Mt. Laundry, having just tackled Mt. Dishes. Taking a deep breath, I start the climb, but just as I feel that I've reached the summit, I realize I'm in a mountain range—and there are more to climb tomorrow. Looking behind me, I see the clouds of car-pool/homeroom and work-outside-the-home duties gathering, and I realize my backpack (the calendar) might explode from overuse.

When I feel overwhelmed in the midst of the endurance test called parenthood, it helps me to remember that I'm not alone—other climbers have gone before me.

In Exodus, the Israelites felt stuck as they followed Moses around the desert. Remember when their enemies were in hot pursuit, and in front of them stood an enormous expanse of water? If they turned back, their rivals would surely kill them. To venture into the Red Sea meant certain death, as well.

Like petulant children, the former slaves turned to the man in charge and whined. I must admit I've done the same thing—many times. But I've found that sometimes God allows us to get to a "stuck place" (like the bottom of an impossible-looking mountain or the shore of the Red Sea) to show His glory to us.

My friend Beth spent several years as a single mom to three girls after her husband died suddenly from a heart attack. She did an amazing job raising them (they are all beautiful, godly young women), but she says it was sometimes excruciatingly lonely.

"One night, I was so tired and overwhelmed that I sobbed on my bed, asking God to *please* send me someone with arms. Even though I treasured my relationship with Jesus and leaned on Him daily, at that point I needed more than His spiritual presence. I needed a physical reminder of His love."

God answered Beth in a miraculous way—as He did with the Israelites. For His chosen people, He sent a mighty wind, which blew back the Red Sea. For His chosen child Beth, He sent a gentle wind of love and comfort.

"Suddenly," Beth says, "I looked over at the rocking chair in my room. It was rocking on its own. And there was a tangible sense of peace that enveloped me. I slept peacefully, and when I woke up, the chair stopped rocking."

Hard to believe? Maybe. But the God who parted the Red Sea is still the same God today. And when we cry out to Him, He answers—sometimes with a miracle, but always with His presence.

Do you feel as if you're climbing an impossible peak with no Sherpa and little oxygen? Does everyday life threaten to swallow up your sanity—or your sense of self?

It might help to remember that the best prayer sometimes is simple: "Help me, Lord!" and that He always answers our cries for assistance.

Especially when we're stuck on the side of a mountain.

Notes from the Coach

*And when the Israelites saw the great power the L*ord
displayed against the Egyptians,
*the people feared the L*ord
and put their trust in him
and in Moses his servant.

E*xodus* 14:31 niv

He makes me as surefooted as a deer,
leading me safely along the mountain heights.

P*salm* 18:33 nlt

He rebuked the Red Sea so that it dried up on the spot—
he paraded them right through!—
no one so much as got wet feet!
He saved them from a life of oppression,
pried them loose from the grip of the enemy.
Then the waters flowed back on their oppressors;
there wasn't a single survivor.
Then they believed his words were true
and broke out in songs of praise.

P*salm* 106:9–12 msg

Treasures in the Darkness

> *Stars may be seen from the bottom of*
> *a deep well when they cannot be discerned from*
> *the top of a mountain.*

CHARLES H. SPURGEON

I have a "deep well" in my life—depression. But I've also seen the stars (God's goodness) from the bottom of the well.

My journey with the disease began after I experienced a miscarriage. I didn't recover from the grief as quickly as I wanted to, and I couldn't figure out why. In the months after my pregnancy loss, Carey changed jobs, we moved, several friends relocated, and my writing career stalled out. When I started to experience panic attacks, I knew I needed help.

Because Carey and I were trying to conceive, I didn't immediately go on medication (later, I started on an anti-depressant, and it has been a tremendous help). Instead, I first went to a Christian counselor, who helped me work through past hurts and faulty thinking patterns.

Knowing myself better was the first gift God gave me through the trial of depression. I used to be constantly busy with ministry tasks, but I was always tired and often frustrated by lack of time with my husband and child. Through counseling, I learned that being busy didn't make God love me more, and I practiced saying no to things that didn't interest, excite, or challenge me. Since I now know my calling (to be a mom, wife, and writer) and my limits, I find that the activities I do participate in are much more fulfilling.

Another of the riches I found in the secret place of depression was a better relationship with Carey. Many times after my counseling sessions, I came out tear-streaked but peaceful; and when Carey asked me questions, I tried to be as honest as possible. The more we talked, the stronger our relationship became.

I also found that depression brought me into a new level of intimacy with God. As I faced each lie I had believed and replaced it with the truth of His Word, I began to experience a sweet closeness in my relationship with the Lord. Sometimes, when I felt like I couldn't walk another step of the arduous journey, He seemed to literally carry me.

Martha Manning's book *Undercurrents*, in which she writes about her life-threatening depression, resonated with me. In a profoundly moving section of the book, Manning has an epiphany in—of all places—the tea aisle of the grocery store. She realizes that her former enemy, depression, has gifted her with a new attitude toward everyday blessings, and that hardships can help anyone become more sensitive to the delightfully mundane, yet wonderful, moments in life.

The final gift of depression has been just such an "increased sensitivity to light." There are moments in my day-to-day life that almost seem to hum with glory. I wasn't in tune with that frequency before, and so I don't take it for granted.

I wouldn't wish depression on my worst enemy, but through my struggle with the disease, I have seen that God uses everything in our lives—even the excruciating suffering we fight so hard against—to bring us closer to Him. And that makes me supremely thankful.

NOTES FROM THE COACH

"I will give you the treasures of darkness,
riches stored in secret places,
so that you may know that I am the LORD,
the God of Israel, who summons you by name."

ISAIAH 45:3 NIV

And we know that in all things
God works for the good of those who love him,
who have been called according to his purpose.

ROMANS 8:28 NIV

"You're blessed when you're at the end of your rope.
With less of you there is more of God and his rule.
You're blessed when you feel you've lost
what is most dear to you.
Only then can you be embraced by
the One most dear to you."

MATTHEW 5:3-4 MSG

They that wait upon the LORD shall renew their strength;
they shall mount up with wings as eagles;
they shall run, and not be weary;
and they shall walk, and not faint.

ISAIAH 40:31 KJV

Welcome Home

Friendship is one of the sweetest joys of life.
Many might have failed beneath the bitterness of
their trial had they not found a friend.

CHARLES H. SPURGEON

"Welcome home, Carey and Dena!" the note on our front door read.

"What's this?" I asked my husband, and he just grinned.

As we stepped into our tiny apartment, my mouth hung open. The place was sparkling—not an ounce of clutter or dust anywhere.

It was 1:30 a.m. As first-year seminary students, Carey and I had spent the past week working at our day jobs and then wolfing down fast food in the car while driving to rehearsals for a Christian theater production.

Ironically, this week was called "hell week" by the cast, since we were only a few days from the show's opening. The 150-member cast and crew spent evenings from 7 to 11 p.m. (or later) going over our movements, getting costumes fitted, and practicing our scenes.

Each day, we had guzzled caffeine at our day jobs and told ourselves it would only last a few more nights. Exhausted, Carey and I assured each other we'd clean our house and car later. . .after we were back in the land of the living.

Now, dropping my bag, I walked through the living/

dining/kitchen area and noticed that the dishes were done—by hand, since we didn't have a dishwasher. The living room floor had been vacuumed, and the linoleum in the cracker-box kitchen had been swept and mopped.

"Who did this?" I asked Carey. He shrugged and laughed.

I made my way into the bedroom, where the bed had been made. A note, taped to the pillow, read: "Enjoy, you lovebirds!"

"It was Andrea and Lee, wasn't it?" I asked. "She must have borrowed the key from you."

Carey nodded. "She asked me for it yesterday, but she wouldn't tell me what she was up to—only that they were planning a surprise."

The Chitwoods and Hartigs, our best friends, were two young married seminary couples from our church.

Though they had all been happy for us when we both got cast in *The Promise*, they were somewhat disappointed when they found out that we'd be tied up on weekends for six months.

But instead of pouting, they lifted a burden for us. They showed us the true meaning of friendship. I'm supremely grateful for burden-lifters like our seminary buddies.

Though both couples moved away several years ago (and we remained behind), God has since met our need for new friends with other families. These friends, too, have often come through for us in a pinch—when we needed a last-minute babysitter, or we had a medical emergency, or if we just needed a safe place to "chill" or "vent." And we try to do the same for them.

As George Eliot once said, "What do we live for if it is not to make life less difficult for each other?"

Amen.

*Let's see how inventive we can be in
encouraging love and helping out,
not avoiding worshiping together as some do
but spurring each other on,
especially as we see the big Day approaching.*

HEBREWS 10:24–25 MSG

"One should be kind to a fainting friend."

JOB 6:14 NLT

*You will be made rich in every way so that
you can be generous on every occasion,
and through us your generosity will result in
thanksgiving to God.*

2 CORINTHIANS 9:11 NIV

*Serve wholeheartedly,
as if you were serving the Lord, not men,
because you know that the Lord will reward
everyone for whatever good he does.*

EPHESIANS 6:7–8 NIV

Never Alone

He who abandons himself to God
will never be abandoned by God.

Source Unknown

Do you sometimes feel utterly alone as a mom—like when the baby's been up all night and your spouse leaves for work? Perhaps that lonely feeling hits when you haven't heard from your best friend in over a month, or you have to stay home with a sick child (again!) while your hubby takes your oldest to church.

At moments like those, I'm comforted by the memory of a trip I took in college and the life-changing lesson I brought home. . . .

Barely twenty years old, I was serving as a summer youth minister in Germany. We had just finished a week-long stint at a camp in Switzerland, and as I hung up the phone and turned to face the kids in my youth group, my face was pale.

"There was a miscommunication," I said. "No one's coming to pick us up."

I explained that two sets of parents each thought the other was driving to pick up the church group—five American military kids and myself—from the week of recreation and worship.

Breathing a prayer for wisdom, I fought back the tears. We had waited at our pickup spot for several hours but finally talked to one of the youth's parents by phone. I would have to stay with the kids—and get them all home—by myself.

As we all walked the short distance to the train terminal, carrying our sleeping bags and suitcases, I kept thinking I was in a bad dream. The trip home would take all night, and we'd have to change trains three times.

"Lord, how can I do this?" I prayed. *"I don't speak any of the languages of any of the countries we're passing through. What if we get on the wrong train?"* I didn't want to be responsible for the five teenagers in my care—I wanted *my* mommy.

After we boarded our first train, I tried to relax. For some reason, the first leg we were booked in a first-class cabin. We sat in luxurious seats at large picture windows.

As the train took off, we passed over a crystal-clear lake that reflected the setting sun. The Swiss Alps towered over the lake, and the sight looked like a postcard I had bought earlier that week.

And suddenly, I felt inexplicable peace. I knew I wasn't really alone. The Creator of those beautiful mountains was beside me, comforting and guiding me.

That night, we made all of our train changes just fine. And I took a powerful lesson away from the experience.

As a mom, I often feel ill-equipped and overwhelmed by the jobs I have to perform: diapering, counseling, carpooling, feeding, bathing, and disciplining, just to name a few. And sometimes, I don't want to be a mommy—I want my own mommy.

But the train trip through Europe reminds me that God is by my side as I "ride the rails" of parenthood. He is a constant, calming presence in my life—even through the many changes that children bring.

And when I look up from my circumstances and remember the Creator, I am assured, once again, that I'm never truly alone.

Notes from the Coach

"I am with you and will watch over you wherever you go,
and I will bring you back to this land.
I will not leave you until I have done
what I have promised you."

Genesis 28:15 NIV

Be brave and strong!
Don't be afraid of the nations
on the other side of the Jordan.
The Lord your God will always be at your side,
and he will never abandon you.

Deuteronomy 31:6 CEV

"I will not leave you as orphans; I will come to you."

John 14:18 NASB

You protect me with salvation—armor;
you hold me up with a firm hand,
caress me with your gentle ways.

Psalm 18:35 MSG

*"For I am the LORD, your God, who
takes hold of your right hand and says to you,
Do not fear; I will help you."*

ISAIAH 41:13 NIV

Girlfriends, Tea, and Me 🌺

Friendship asks and wants,
hollows and fills, ages with us and we through it,
and cradles us, finally, like family.

BETH KEPHART

What would I do without my girlfriends? Probably go crazy.

A group of us from church refer to ourselves as the "Ha-Ha Sisterhood," because we laugh so much when we're together. Though we don't have girlfriend gatherings as often as we'd like, when we make the time to go out to eat, play games, or see a chick flick together, we're never sorry.

Our circle has supported each other through trials like depression, health problems, the death of loved ones, difficulties with children, divorce, and job struggles.

And then there are my long-distance friends: buddies from college, pals who have moved away, and writing cohorts whom I met online. They e-mail me with news, call with congratulations, and make me laugh with their newsletters. I'm so glad some of them haven't written me off—especially since I haven't sent Christmas cards in two years!

Friendships like these help me cope. They are truly gifts from God. In her book, *Into the Tangle of Friendship*, Beth Kephart sums up the type of companionship I'm supremely grateful for during this stressful season of motherhood: "Throughout our lives, friends enclose us, like pairs of parentheses. They shift our boundaries, crater our terrain. . . . They are the antidote, not to our aloneness, but to our loneliness."

Last Christmas, I held a thank-you tea at a local tearoom for my buddies. We each brought a basket of some sort to exchange, and we had scones and clotted cream (it tastes better than it sounds!). But mostly, we laughed and reminisced about our year and decided that there is really nothing better than a girlfriend.

In fact, a true gal pal is kind of like a warm cup of tea.

Some of my girlfriends are like Lemon Spice tea—extroverts who enjoy being the center of attention. They're fun, witty, easygoing, optimistic, and outspoken. They laugh easily and can talk to anyone at anytime—even if they've just met them.

Other friends are more like Chamomile tea. They're introverted, soft-spoken, laid-back, and great listeners. I love their calming presence in stressful times, their dry wit, and the way they wait to speak until they have something profound to share.

And then there are my Orange Spice buddies—outgoing, optimistic organizers. They love to be in charge and are decisive and goal-oriented. I admire their zest for life, adventurous spirit, and "take-charge" mentality.

I'm more of an Earl Grey gal, and I have a few friends who are like me—an organized, soft-spoken introvert who likes space and solitude. Though we may try to control situations with our dark moods, we're supremely loyal, dependable, and persistent.

I'm extremely thankful for each of my friends. These ladies enrich my life with lunches, notes, road trips, hugs, and girl talk. God has used them as counselors, cheerleaders, and even coaches—to encourage me when I'm down, support me when I'm stressed, rejoice with me when I'm feeling triumphant, and bring me down a few notches when I need it.

In their own ways, they each suit me to a "tea"!

Notes from the Coach

A friend loves at all times,
And a brother is born for adversity.

Proverbs 17:17 NASB

Therefore, as God's chosen people, holy and dearly loved,
clothe yourselves with compassion, kindness,
humility, gentleness and patience.

Colossians 3:12 NIV

The body we're talking about is Christ's body of chosen people.
Each of us finds our meaning and function
as a part of his body.

Romans 12:5 MSG

You are better off to have a friend than to be all alone,
because then you will get more
enjoyment out of what you earn.
If you fall, your friend can help you up.
But if you fall without having a friend nearby,
you are really in trouble. If you sleep alone,
you won't have anyone to keep you warm on a cold night.
Someone might be able to beat up one of you,
but not both of you. As the saying goes,
"A rope made from three strands of cord is hard to break."

Ecclesiastes 4:9–12 CEV

SECTION SEVEN

In the
Final Stretch

Forgive—Who, Me?

The more a man knows, the more he forgives.

CATHERINE THE GREAT

When I found out my friend's husband had cheated on her, I wanted to "heap burning coals of fire on his head." (That's biblical, isn't it?) But they worked through their problems and are now back together. She's forgiven him—why can't I?

My friend Tina's brother was murdered soon after 9/11 by a crazed veteran who started shooting people in a hospital cafeteria. I wonder how she'll ever get past that act of senseless violence.

I question how children who've been abused can forgive their abusers. I struggle to understand what possesses a husband to allow his wife to come home after she's had an affair. And how do you forgive someone who—God forbid!—hurts your own child?

If you've been betrayed or rejected, what kind of grace does God give that enables you to grow beyond it and not become embittered for life? I know it's possible—I've seen it happen. I've even forgiven some of those hurts in my own life, through lots of tears and prayers. However, the process is still mostly a mystery to me.

Usually, forgiveness seems as difficult as getting into a pair of my jeans from high school. I tend to nurse my grudges like a feverish child, fretting over them and tending to them carefully—but to keep them ill, not heal them.

That's really sad, I know. But it's the way I am.

I *want* to be like Corrie ten Boom, who endured innumerable atrocities at the hands of the Nazis during World War II, and later—with the help of God—absolved her enemies. In *Tramp for the Lord*, she wrote, "Forgiveness is not an emotion. . .[it's] an act of the will, and the will can function regardless of the temperature of the heart."

That makes sense to me. I may not feel like forgiving, but that doesn't mean God's commands don't apply to me.

It helps me to remember all the times I've been forgiven. My husband forgives me when I make a sarcastic remark during a fight, my children forgive me when I lose my temper after they've tried my patience one too many times, and my friends forgive me when I don't call or write as often as I should.

And God forgives me daily, for all sorts of alarming behaviors: lustful thoughts, greediness, selfishness, laziness, failure to pray, harboring doubts, worrying about things He's already taken care of—the list could go on, but I'm not enjoying writing it!

It also helped me immensely when my counselor told me, "Forgiveness is not excusing the behavior. It's more complicated than that. What the person did to you was wrong, and you need to admit that before you can move on."

I truly believe that forgiving others (and maybe ourselves, too) is one of the hardest things we have to do as Christians. But if we don't follow God's commands, what's our faith for? What kind of example do we set for a hurting world? Not a very good one, I'm afraid.

This is the part of forgiveness I *do* understand: If we take the first step, God will meet us—and lead us—from there.

Notes from the Coach

" 'This is what you are to say to Joseph:
I ask you to forgive your brothers the sins
and the wrongs they committed in treating you so badly.'
Now please forgive the sins of the servants
of the God of your father."
When their message came to him, Joseph wept.

Genesis 50:17 niv

"Listen to the supplication of Your servant
and of Your people Israel,
when they pray toward this place;
hear in heaven Your dwelling place;
hear and forgive."

1 Kings 8:30 nasb

O my soul,
bless God, don't forget a single blessing!
He forgives your sins—every one.

Psalm 103:2–3 msg

[Jesus said,] If you forgive others
for the wrongs they do to you,
your Father in heaven will forgive you.

But if you don't forgive others,
your Father will not forgive your sins.

MATTHEW 6:14–15 CEV

Then Peter came to Him and said,
"Lord, how often shall my brother sin against me,
and I forgive him? Up to seven times?"
Jesus said to him,
"I do not say to you, up to seven times,
but up to seventy times seven."

MATTHEW 18:21–22 NKJV

He'll Never Reject Us!

*Let me have the courage to live fully even when it is risky,
vibrantly even when it leads to pain,
and spontaneously even when it leads to mistakes.*

HENRI NOUWEN

In high school, a friend experienced a devastating loss involving a family member and was then told by her grandfather, "I'm glad you got the wind knocked out of you. You've always been a Pollyanna." Ouch!

Rejection—we've all experienced it. Some days, it seems to roll off our backs; and on others, we feel as if a knife just pierced our vital organs. Sometimes the risks involved with relationships don't seem worth it, do they?

Maybe you've been shunned by a friend, coworker, or employer. Perhaps you've experienced an even deeper-cutting rejection by a spouse or a loved one. Or maybe, for whatever reason, you're the one who's done the rejecting.

I once got a phone call from a friend at church, who thought I'd been talking behind her back. She felt hurt and rightly so. I was upset that she believed I had betrayed her. But I was grateful that instead of ignoring me or spreading rumors, she came to me so we could talk the situation out. As a matter of fact, we're good friends to this day.

As a freelance writer, I experience rejection of my ideas and projects on a weekly basis. At times, it's hard not to take those letters, which all sound remarkably similar, personally. When I was trying to break into the book market (something that took five years of learning, growing, praying, and waiting—after several years of writing articles and stories for freelance markets), the multiple rejections got to me after awhile.

Even though I believed I was called to write and felt that I was being obedient to God by pursuing that call, major discouragement set in for me when three of my favorite publishers turned down a nonfiction book proposal *in one week*. Ouch again!

My husband, friends, and family encouraged me to keep going. And I wanted to—but my "fight" was running out. The rewards of risk just didn't seem worth it anymore.

Then God gave me a gift—a passage from Eugene Peterson's *The Message* (1 Thessalonians 5:9–24), at the precise moment I needed it. I hope it will minister to you as it did to me:

> "God didn't set us up for an angry *rejection* but for salvation by our Master, Jesus Christ. . . . So speak encouraging words to one another. Build up hope so you'll all be together in this. . . . Be cheerful no matter what; pray all the time; thank God no matter what happens. . . . The One who called you is completely dependable. If he said it, he'll do it!"

Isn't that awesome? Those verses remind me that God is up to great things behind the scenes. That truth allows me to build up hope, so that I can get back into the ring of life and keep fighting—for relationships, for a vibrant life, and for the calling God has placed on my life.

Another truth that helps me keep on keeping on is this: Even when friends, family members, or publishers reject me,

Jesus never does. And God's acceptance makes me willing to keep living life fully, even when it's risky.

NOTES FROM THE COACH

*"Yet in spite of this,
when they are in the land of their enemies,
I will not reject them or abhor them
so as to destroy them completely,
breaking my covenant with them.
I am the LORD their God."*

LEVITICUS 26:44 NIV

*"For the sake of his great name the LORD
will not reject his people,
because the LORD was pleased to make you his own."*

1 SAMUEL 12:22 NIV

*No more will anyone call you Rejected,
and your country will no more be called Ruined.
You'll be called Hephzibah (My Delight),
and your land Beulah (Married),
Because GOD delights in you and your land
will be like a wedding celebration.*

ISAIAH 62:4 MSG

"I took you from the ends of the earth,
from its farthest corners I called you.
I said, 'You are my servant';
I have chosen you and have not rejected you."

ISAIAH 41:9 NIV

But you are the ones chosen by God,
chosen for the high calling of priestly work,
chosen to be a holy people,
God's instruments to do his work and speak out for him,
to tell others of the night-and-day
difference he made for you—
from nothing to something, from rejected to accepted.

1 PETER 2:9–10 MSG

Birthdays and Other Blowouts

Our life is frittered away by detail...simplify, simplify!

HENRY DAVID THOREAU

Is it just me, or are kids' birthday parties becoming too extravagant? Growing up, all we needed was pin-the-tail-on-the-donkey, some cake and ice cream, and a few favors. Now, moms feel pressured to have an overarching theme, live entertainment, bounce houses, and pony rides—not to mention goody bags rivaling those given to Academy Award presenters.

One woman I know takes the "theme" concept to the nth degree. For her daughter's Wizard of Oz party, each family member dressed up as a different character from the movie. This supermom created a yellow brick road and mini Emerald City in her backyard, hung flying monkeys from the trees, and had a professional photographer there to capture every "Over the Rainbow" moment. (I'm not making this up!) I think she stopped short of bringing in munchkins for atmosphere, though I'm not sure.

Kind of puts my ninety-nine-cent package of Buzz Light-year napkins to shame.

But more power to her, I say—and to you, if your idea of fun is creating elaborate spectacles for little people. I'd rather spend my time and money in other ways. Have you ever gone overboard in your quest to outdo all your friends and put on the ultimate birthday bash? You know you've gone too far when. . .

- You have to take out a loan (or rack up charges on your credit card) to fund the party.
- Instead of enjoying the celebration, you spend the entire time with tight shoulders and a sick stomach, anticipating a breakdown in the party structure.
- You've set up a flowchart of party activities that can only be deviated from in an emergency (and you have strict definitions of the word *emergency*).
- You have to hire a staff to take care of all the details you've planned.
- You're exhausted after it ends and vow to never do it again.

A minister at my church said recently, "Simplicity is a lost art." I think he's right—and I believe our obsession with having "be-all and end-all" parties for our children is just a symptom of a larger cultural malady.

Major holidays—from birthdays to Christmas, Easter to Valentine's—have become ways to show how extravagant and creative we can be, instead of days to honor family, friends, and faith. It's up to us as parents—especially Christian parents—to say "enough is enough" and get back to basics. Let's begin to value simplicity, and maybe others will follow our lead.

It's not that I want to ignore birthdays and holidays—quite the opposite. I think special times should be celebrated with vim, vigor, and gusto (not to mention lots of chocolate). I just believe we should concentrate more on celebrating the persons in our lives—our precious gifts from God—instead of glorifying our ability to plan (and pay for) a big blowout.

Now, who wants some cake?

NOTES FROM THE COACH

A pretentious, showy life is an empty life;
a plain and simple life is a full life.

PROVERBS 13:7 MSG

"Martha, Martha," the Lord answered,
"you are worried and upset about many things,
but only one thing is needed."

LUKE 10:41–42 NIV

Now godliness with contentment is great gain.

1 TIMOTHY 6:6 NKJV

Not that I speak in respect of want:
for I have learned, in whatsoever state I am,
therein to be content.
I know how to be abased,
and I know also how to abound:
in everything and in all things have I learned
the secret both to be filled and to be hungry,
both to abound and to be in want.

PHILIPPIANS 4:11–12 ASV

All About Love

Marriage will either drive you crazy, or to Christ.

ANONYMOUS

Like most women, I'm a sucker for romance.

I love Valentine's Day, flowers, jewelry, and dinners on the town. I like to read novels by Francine Rivers and Jan Karon, and I even sneak a peek at the final episodes of dating shows like *The Bachelor*, hoping unrealistically that people might just find lasting love with a camera stuck in their face.

In fact, when I was eleven years old, I voraciously read every book in a series of teen romances. And as a budding author, I naively thought, *I could write one of these!*

I ended up writing two. The titles of my titillating novels? *Magical Daydreams* and *Someday, Somewhere* (gag!). I had no luck getting them published—not enough life experience with the subject matter, I suppose.

But I still held out hope that I would have my own romance someday, and I prayed for a Prince Charming. Imagine my surprise when that answered prayer and I had our first fight in the car, driving away from our dream wedding! He wanted to stop and clean the car of its "Just Married" debris—from top to bottom, mind you—while I was ready to hose it down quickly and get to our destination, which was still an hour's drive away. Our second fight, which took place a week later in our newlywed apartment, was about how to organize the refrigerator. Can you say "obsessive-compulsive"?

Come to think of it, most of our fusses have been about preferences over cleanliness and order—which I'm thankful for. We share similar values, backgrounds, and passions, so we don't fight a lot. And he's, quite simply, a wonderful husband.

But my idea of "wedded bliss" was *not* being in tears on the way to our honeymoon suite.

Maybe you've had a similar wake-up call. Marriage tends to give us those, doesn't it? No matter how much our husband loves us—or we love him—he's never going to be "enough" to satisfy our little-girl longings for a knight in shining armor.

That's why I love two books God placed in my path over the last few years: *The Sacred Romance* by John Eldredge and Brent Curtis and *The Allure of Hope* by Jan Meyers. Instead of giving "quick fix" answers to a woman's heartaches and questions ("Is this all there is?" and "Why do I want more all the time?"), they maintain that our longing for beauty and perfection isn't wrong—just misplaced.

Meyers writes, "Living with childlike faith brings the subtle ache that does not go away. The groaning comes from unlimited vision of what could be. . .[and] hope is something that rises up inside of us with a gentle strength that requires a response. We either respond to it with our hearts or we try to push it down."

In other words, we can shut down our longings (which might be more comfortable in the beginning), or we can go to God with them, and let Him show us what we're truly wanting.

You know what I've found? *He* is a fault-free Bridegroom, and—amazing as this is—He calls me His "Beloved."

How's that for romantic?

Notes from the Coach

He has taken me to the banquet hall,
and his banner over me is love.

Song of Song 2:4 niv

For your royal husband delights in your beauty;
honor him, for he is your lord.

Psalm 45:11 nlt

"For your Maker is your bridegroom,
his name, God-of-the-Angel-Armies!
Your Redeemer is The Holy of Israel,
known as God of the whole earth."

Isaiah 54:5 msg

I promise that from that day on,
you will call me your husband instead of your master.

Hosea 2:16 cev

"Let the beloved of the Lord rest secure in him,
for he shields [her] all day long,
and the one the Lord loves rests between his shoulders."

Deuteronomy 33:12 niv

Dancing in the Frozen-Food Aisle

Dance like no one is watching.

Lindsay Kolb

On my mother's side, I come from a long line of "creatives." Which is a nice way of saying our family is a little whacked-out.

My great-grandfather wrote tons of unpublished short stories, some of which I have. His daughter, Nanaw, was an artist and writer, as well as an art teacher. Her husband, Dadaw, was an amateur inventor and held several patents before he died. And my mother is a talented decorator and has published a few stories of her own.

I love my nontypical bloodline. But I have noticed that sometimes the craziness inherent in creative people comes at the expense of their family members' comfort.

For instance, Nanaw and Dadaw used to dance to the Muzak in the grocery store, much to my mother's chagrin. While they waltzed around the frozen food, she hid behind the stacks of canned goods, praying no one would see her. Their defense? "We can't let this good music go to waste!"

I know I've been an embarrassment—and a frustration—to my darling hubby at times. (I will be to my son, too, as soon as he's old enough to realize I'm not "normal.") Even though my husband is a professional entertainer, he tends to keep his creativity at work. I, on the other hand, love to decorate and redecorate. In fact, Carey never knows when he'll come home to a totally different house than the one he left that morning!

He loves to tell people about my goofs, too—like the afternoon I decided our office wall could use some inspirational art. Instead of taking the time to find a stencil, I proceeded to freehand on the wall, with a Magic Marker, a "feel-good" quote about writing. (Hey, it looked oh-so-easy and oh-so-lovely when Lynette Jennings did it on HGTV.)

My version looked horrible, although I did cover it up nicely with a quilt. However, Carey often pulls up the blanket to show visitors the "artwork" on the office wall, as if to say, "Look what I put up with!"

To be fair, Carey also brags on me incessantly and says my wacky side keeps our marriage fun and interesting. Recently, when I told him I had always wanted to go to circus camp and learn the trapeze, his mouth dropped open and he shook his head. "We've been married ten years, and you just now tell me this?" he asked. "Honey, I love you. . .but I'll never understand you."

At least he'll never get bored!

In fact, he encouraged me to write about my grandparents dancing in the aisles. "What a great story!" he said. "You have to write that down."

And I do love the mental picture of Nanaw and Dadaw shunning convention and kicking up their heels in the middle of "Thrift-Mart," especially since I never really knew my grandfather. I know he suffered from depression, and I know he basically worried himself to death at a relatively young age.

But somehow, in the grocery store, my grandmother's influence over him—or his own sense of absurdity—helped him let go of his worries and embrace life.

Maybe the next time I go shopping, I'll do the same.

Notes from the Coach

Then Miriam the prophetess, Aaron's sister,
took a tambourine in her hand,
and all the women followed her,
with tambourines and dancing.

Exodus 15:20 NIV

David retorted to Michal,
"I was dancing before the LORD,
who chose me above your father and his family!
He appointed me as the leader of Israel,
the people of the LORD.
So I am willing to act like a fool
in order to show my joy in the LORD."

2 Samuel 6:21 NLT

I scrub my hands with purest soap,
then join hands with the others in the great circle,
dancing around your altar, GOD.

Psalm 26:6 MSG

You have turned my sorrow into joyful dancing.
No longer am I sad and wearing sackcloth.

Psalm 30:11 CEV

The castoffs of society will be
*laughing and dancing in G*OD,
the down-and-outs shouting praise
to The Holy of Israel.

ISAIAH 29:19 MSG

SECTION EIGHT

Crossing the Finish Line

Psalm 23 for Today

God's guidance is
even more important than common sense...
I can declare that the deepest darkness
is outshone by the light of Jesus.

CORRIE TEN BOOM

As I sat on the couch, I opened the *USA Today*. Inside the front section was an article detailing the ways to prepare for all sorts of terrorist attacks. As I read, visions of duct tape and plastic sheeting danced in my head, and the fact that I live a mere twenty miles from a nuclear power plant crossed my mind more than once.

Then I tried to go to bed. Right. (What was I thinking!)

But after I crawled in the covers, with my mind swirling and my heart racing, I looked up my daily reading in a devotional book. As God's providence would have it, the selection was Psalm 23. And as I read, I realized the words were timeless. They comforted me, and I began to think of ways that they might apply to our current situation in America.

Here's what I recorded that night in my journal:

The Lord is my Shepherd—
In the midst of the war on drugs,
the war on terrorism,
and the spiritual warfare in my soul.

I shall not want—
with Him as my Savior and provider,
I'm perfectly content.
While others strive for and worry about
a bigger house, a newer car, designer clothes, and jewels,
I will rest in my calling and purpose—
knowing God and making Him known
in this hurting, harried world.

He leads me beside still waters—
Cool, clear streams of peace
in the midst of orange alerts,
space shuttle disasters, stock market fluctuations,
and baggage inspections.
When emotional baggage threatens my sanity,
He renews my mind.
When grief and despair descend,
He heals my heart.
When doubts and fears assail my tranquillity,
He restores my soul.

Yea, though I walk through the valley
of the shadow of death—
filled with threats of biological and chemical warfare,
nuclear bombs and ghosts of past regrets—
I will fear no evil.
Not AIDS or smallpox,
not child abductors or doomsayers.
Thou art with me—
even when I feel alone in a crowd.

Thy rod and Thy staff, they comfort me—
especially when I read the paper or watch the news.

(Why do I read or watch? I know the ending!)
Thou anointest my head with oil—
the oil of gladness and peace,
with a calling to be
light and joy in a dark, fear-filled world.

Help me to be a peace-full, grace-full person, Lord,
in the midst of a chaotic world.
Truly, my cup runneth over.
You have blessed me so much!
I have friends and family who love me,
a warm bed, freedom, grace, (more than) enough food,
and a fulfilling purpose.

Surely goodness and mercy—
Your grace, love, forgiveness, and compassion—
shall follow me all the days of my life.
Every second, every minute, You are before and
behind me, with Your arms of love outstretched.

And one day—when all wars and pain,
terror and shame
will come to an end. . .(Come quickly, Lord Jesus!)
I will dwell in the house of the Lord,
Your glorious kingdom,
where You've prepared an eternal home for me.

As I finished the psalm, I turned out the light and went
to sleep. Peacefully.

NOTES FROM THE COACH

A PSALM OF DAVID.
The LORD is my shepherd, I shall not be in want.
He makes me lie down in green pastures,
he leads me beside quiet waters,
he restores my soul.
He guides me in paths of righteousness
for his name's sake.
Even though I walk
through the valley of the shadow of death,
I will fear no evil,
for you are with me;
your rod and your staff,
they comfort me.
You prepare a table before me
in the presence of my enemies.
You anoint my head with oil;
my cup overflows.
Surely goodness and love will follow me
all the days of my life,
and I will dwell in the house of the LORD forever.

PSALM 23 NIV

The Cat's Meow

Oh, beloved nap time, nature's soft nurse.

WILLIAM SHAKESPEARE

All of my best friends own cats. Now, that may not seem like a big deal to you, but get this: I'm so allergic to cats that I wheeze just looking at them. If I'm in a house with multiple felines, you'd better have 9-1-1 on speed-dial.

But lately I've found out (from online research—you didn't think I'd do it in *person,* did you?) that cats can be good for you. Scientists have actually proven that pets reduce stress in their owners.

I'm not suggesting you run out and adopt the nearest stray. However, I *am* advising you to inventory your daily habits and stress levels. Why? Because if we busy moms are not healthy—emotionally, spiritually, and physically—then our mates, kids, coworkers, and friends will be the second ones who feel it (right after *we* feel it).

In 1 Corinthians 6:19–20 (NIV), Paul writes: "Do you not know that your body is a temple of the Holy Spirit. . . ? You were bought at a price. Therefore honor God with your body."

Several years ago, I was diagnosed with an underactive thyroid. And believe it or not, it's a gift. This illness, which often leads to fatigue when I overdo or under-rest, forces me to have healthy habits.

Here are a few "catty" things I can no longer do without:

CATNAPS

I nap when I can—and that means when my husband is caring for our young sons or I have a break at work. Naps have helped me make it through the rest of the day on many occasions.

CAT FOOD

I've found that my body does much better when I feed it plenty of fruits and vegetables, lean meats, little or no sugar and caffeine, and lots of water. (This is a daily struggle for someone like me, who grew up on T-bone steaks. When your dad's a cattle rancher, you don't eat a lot of chicken!)

CAT STRETCHES

I have always disliked exercising. . .almost as much as I loathed being around cats. But staying active helps me feel better emotionally. I now try to exercise at least three times a week, and I feel it when I don't. Exercising gives me energy, instead of taking it.

That leads me to my last, and undeniably favorite, "Category" about taking care of myself:

CAT SCRATCHES

- Have you ever had an hour-long, energy-giving, relaxing-to-the-core massage—complete with soft music and candles? If not, you're missing out. Listen, I truly love my family's affections, but I'm not above paying for a good kneading of my muscles now and then. That hour of being pampered is *so* worth the expense.
- If massages aren't for you, try rocking your child to sleep or cuddling with your spouse at the end of the day. Have your teenage daughter rub your hands with lotion, and then return the favor.

As you'll discover, tender touches—and all these other aspects of self-care—are definitely the cat's meow.

Notes from the Coach

And let me live whole and holy, soul and body,
so I can always walk with my head held high.

Psalm 119:80 msg

Those who discover these words live, really live;
body and soul, they're bursting with health.

Proverbs 4:22 msg

Since we have these promises, dear friends,
let us purify ourselves from everything that
contaminates body and spirit,
perfecting holiness out of reverence for God.

2 Corinthians 7:1 niv

May God himself, the God who makes everything holy
and whole, make you holy and whole, put you together—
spirit, soul, and body—
and keep you fit for the coming of
our Master, Jesus Christ.

1 Thessalonians 5:23 msg

Can I Get a Witness?

*Success is never final and failure is never fatal.
It's courage that counts.*

GEORGE TILTON

My father used to lead the music at a Southern Baptist church, which meant that growing up, we attended church twice on Sundays, once on Wednesdays, and again on Tuesday evenings for "visitation." (Have you heard the not-too-far-from-the-truth rhyme about our denomination? "Mary had a little lamb; it would have been a sheep—but she joined the Southern Baptist church and died from lack of sleep!")

I always dreaded Tuesdays, especially after I "aged out" of the nursery, because visitation meant going door-to-door in pairs, witnessing to people.

Gulp. Although I became a Christian at age seven, as a teenager I was hesitant to talk about Jesus. And every week, I tried to come up with excuses not to go "visiting." Sometimes, I was successful. Mostly, I took part—miserably.

There was at least once, however, when I became bold about sharing my faith. In 1983 at a Christian youth camp, I became burdened about one of the boys in our group. Eric wasn't born again, and I knew God wanted him to accept Christ. I decided *I* was the one to help him.

So I roped him into going for a walk. Then I went into the "spiel" I had practiced during my long years of witnessing training.

"I've heard this before," he growled as I began, "and I don't want your Jesus!"

Then he (literally) ran off.

I sat there, stunned. I was crushed. What did I do wrong? I thought my heart was right with God. Did I push too hard?

It was years before I would verbally witness again. I decided I would let my light shine through my actions and allow people to ask me questions if they wanted the joy and peace I had. The only problem was that no one ever asked.

Recently, I ran across the motto of that Christian camp: "Successful witnessing is sharing Christ through the power of the Holy Spirit and leaving the results to God." That resonated with me, since I still don't know what became of Eric.

Over several years of being a nonwitness, I realized that I wasn't being obedient to Christ's mandate to share the gospel with the world. And I began to look for opportunities to talk about Jesus in a natural way.

I still don't witness nearly as much as I should. Sometimes when I do, I fall on my face. Always, I feel nervous, but I know God is proud of me for "just trying."

Recently, I shared Christ with a friend of mine. I had prayed for an opportunity to talk to him for several months. When he asked me about something spiritual, I set up a time to talk with him later, at length. Then I called every Christian friend I knew and asked them to pray like crazy.

During our conversation, I was uncharacteristically calm—through the power of the Holy Spirit. God brought several scriptures to mind that I hadn't planned on bringing up. Through it all, I felt peaceful, even joyful.

And now, I'm leaving the results to God.

NOTES FROM THE COACH

"In the same way,
let your light shine before men,
that they may see your good deeds
and praise your Father in heaven."

MATTHEW 5:16 NIV

Go to the people of all nations and make them
my disciples. Baptize them in the name of the Father,
the Son, and the Holy Spirit,
and teach them to do everything I have told you.
I will be with you always, even until the end of the world.

MATTHEW 28:19–20 CEV

Go out into the world uncorrupted,
a breath of fresh air in this squalid and polluted society.
Provide people with a glimpse of good living
and of the living God.
Carry the light-giving Message into the night
so I'll have good cause to be proud of you
on the day that Christ returns.
You'll be living proof that I didn't go to
all this work for nothing.

PHILIPPIANS 2:15–16 MSG

Be very careful, then, how you live—
not as unwise but as wise,
making the most of every opportunity,
because the days are evil.

EPHESIANS 5:15–16 NIV

Planting a Garden of Gratitude

Let us be grateful to people who make us happy—
they are the charming gardeners who make our souls blossom.

MARCEL PROUST

Last Christmas, I came across a unique book called *Ferris Wheels, Daffodils, and Hot Fudge Sundaes* by Laura Jensen Walker. This gratitude journal, which was inspired by Walker's bout with breast cancer, consists of blank pages to write on, quotes and scriptures about thankfulness, and her own lists of the things—both big and little—she's grateful for.

One afternoon, Jordan noticed the journal and asked if he could write in it. I thought, *Why not?*

Here's what my five-and-a-half-year-old recorded (spelling errors and translations included): "I'm thankful for. . .santa, baby jesus, momy and dade, mi [my] house, or [our] bones, mi presents, or hort [our heart], luv fum [from] momy and dady, for God, apol jows [apple juice], and I am gad dit we r nt mosdrs [I am glad that we are not monsters]."

Jordan's creative list inspired me to write down some of the things I'm thankful for: God's never-ending patience with me. . .two working vehicles—and one that's paid for. . .a potty-trained child (I thought he was going to be in the *Guinness Book* for oldest kid in diapers!). . .girlfriends. . .the movie *Babette's Feast* and musical *Les Miserable*. . .e-mail. . .gooey chocolate brownies. . .Christian parents. . .good relationships with my in-laws. . .for a husband who cooks, babysits, and does laundry (don't hate me, ladies!). . .and for a mom who made me write thank-you notes after every holiday—before I played with my gifts—and who wrote me affirming letters as I was growing up, listing the things about me she was thankful for.

Come to think of it, my mother was an excellent model of thanksgiving. Even when she went through a lengthy illness, she kept a great attitude. And Jordan's desire to create his own journal page reminded me that gratitude—like many of the attributes we want (or don't want!) our children to develop—can be taught by example. What a scary, but thrilling, idea!

"This, surely, is the most valuable legacy we can pass on to the next generation," wrote Arthur Gordon in *A Touch of Wonder*. "Not money, houses, or heirlooms, but a capacity for wonder and gratitude, a sense of aliveness and joy. Why don't we work harder at it? Probably, because as Thoreau said, our lives are frittered away by details. Because there are times when we don't have the awareness or the selflessness or the energy."

I'm going to start praying for that selflessness, awareness, and energy, so I can plant seeds of gratitude in my children.

Wanna join me? With God's help, maybe even on tough days we can model a spirit of thankfulness to all those around us. And pretty soon, we might be surprised at the beautiful garden of gratitude that has sprung up around us.

NOTES FROM THE COACH

Keep a sharp eye out for weeds of bitter discontent.
A thistle or two gone to seed can ruin
a whole garden in no time.

HEBREWS 12:15 MSG

Then we your people, the sheep of your pasture,
will thank you forever and ever,
praising your greatness from generation to generation.

PSALM 79:13 NLT

Speak to one another with psalms,
hymns and spiritual songs.
Sing and make music in your heart to the Lord,
always giving thanks to God the Father for everything,
in the name of our Lord Jesus Christ.

EPHESIANS 5:19–20 NIV

With all my heart I praise the LORD!
I will never forget how kind he has been.

PSALM 103:2 CEV

And we pray this in order that you may live a life worthy of
the Lord and may please him in every way:
bearing fruit in every good work,
growing in the knowledge of God,
being strengthened with all power according to
his glorious might so that you may have great endurance
and patience, and joyfully giving thanks to the Father,
who has qualified you to share in the inheritance of
the saints in the kingdom of light.

COLOSSIANS 1:10–12 NIV

A Few Choice Words

Eating words has never given me indigestion.

WINSTON CHURCHILL

I blew it, and I knew it.

There I stood, laughing with a friend about one of my husband's faults. Suddenly, he turned the corner and heard my remark. As his face fell, my heart sank.

I had wounded him deeply, and I felt ashamed. Later, I apologized to my husband, and I asked the Lord's forgiveness. Both forgave me, but I never forgot that my words caused a rift—however temporary—in two of my most precious relationships.

That day, I learned the truth of what the Bible says in Proverbs 12:18 (NIV): "Reckless words pierce like a sword, but the tongue of the wise brings healing."

In *Words Begin in Our Hearts*, Rhonda Webb tells this story about her son, Jimmy: "When Jimmy was four, he was constantly talking. One afternoon while driving down a country road near our home. . .I finally cracked, slammed on the brakes, and told him that if he did not stop talking, I would leave him on the side of the road. Well, he quieted down. I drove about five feet and stopped the car again. At this point, we were both crying. I climbed into the backseat, held his hands, told him how sorry I was for speaking to him that way, and asked him to forgive me."

Like Rhonda, I've seen my son's tender heart crushed due

to my harsh words, spoken in a fit of anger. Why do we let the ones we love the most push our buttons the hardest?

If you're like my friends and me, you've also messed up in the "words" department. (And if you think you haven't, you're probably lying to yourself!)

So what's an often-harried mom to do? How can we keep from a) saying anything and everything that comes to mind, to the detriment of people around us, or b) biting our tongues off while dealing with the frustrations of life?

As I've studied scripture and pondered the often-rash remarks that flow out of my mouth, I've discovered I need to pray daily for providential patience. There is simply no way I can always use words the right way without God's help.

Rhonda encourages women—and men—who want to have a more consistent, Christlike flow of speech to be involved in regular personal Bible study, scripture memory, and group Bible study. She also says that her friend Julie taught her a technique they call *fast-forward thinking*. "This is when you think, 'If I say this, what will happen afterward? Will I be glad I said it? Will I wish I could take it back?' "

As you work on gaining control of your tongue, which the Bible compares to a rudder on a ship, it may seem more trouble than it's worth. Getting our words right takes discipline, self-denial, and determination.

But the results (mended relationships and peace of mind) are well worth it. I'll be praying for you—as soon as I pry this size 7 boot out of my mouth.

NOTES FROM THE COACH

A truly wise person uses few words;
a person with understanding is even-tempered.

Even fools are thought to be wise when they keep silent;
when they keep their mouths shut, they seem intelligent.

PROVERBS 17:27–28 NLT

May the words of my mouth and the meditation
of my heart be pleasing in your sight,
O LORD, my Rock and my Redeemer.

PSALM 19:14 NIV

The words of his mouth are wicked and deceitful;
he has ceased to be wise and to do good.

PSALM 36:3 NIV

"Let me tell you something:
Every one of these careless words is
going to come back to haunt you.
There will be a time of Reckoning.
Words are powerful; take them seriously."

MATTHEW 12:36 MSG

Whatever you do in word or deed,
do all in the name of the Lord Jesus,
giving thanks through Him to God the Father.

COLOSSIANS 3:17 NASB

SECTION NINE

On the Podium

A Daring Adventure

To love what you do and feel that it matters,
how could anything be more fun?

KATHERINE GRAHAM

I'm not a thrill seeker by any means. My idea of taking risks includes driving through town with my doors unlocked or (and this is a biggie) putting eleven items on the 10 ITEMS OR LESS express lane at Wal-Mart. So imagine my chagrin when God decided to take me on a thrill ride five years ago. . . .

When our oldest son was a baby, Carey and I used to push his stroller around the park to get some "together" time. One night during our walk, Carey said, "I want to resign."

That wasn't the kind of together time I had been hoping for.

However, I knew Carey was unhappy in his job as a youth minister. He loved the kids, but as the group got larger, so did his administrative responsibilities (not his forte).

I had reservations. Okay, let's be honest—I was petrified. With his job, I felt that we had security: a regular paycheck, health insurance, and a supportive church. I worked part-time as a freelance writer, which doesn't provide a regular salary.

So, for several months we prayed and I cried. My doubts about whether we could make a living outside a typical church setting didn't faze Carey. Full of faith—or foolishness, as my grandmother and other friends believed—he was confident we needed to serve God again through the creative arts. (Years earlier, we had met in a touring Christian music theater group.)

Finally, I gave in. I wish I could say it was out of confidence that God would provide; but mostly He, and Carey, wore me down. And I realized that in order to honor my husband, I needed to support his dreams.

Not even two weeks after telling the pastor about our plan to resign (but before we had announced the decision to our congregation), a couple we had met at church approached us. Russ and Wendy were starting a professional, Christian-owned music theater in our town. "We know you're busy with the youth group, but we'd love your input," they said.

Our jaws dropped. "Actually, we're not going to be that busy," we said. When we told them of our plans, they asked us to perform in their very first production.

That was four and a half years ago. We've been resident cast members ever since. Carey helps write and perform in all the productions. I sing only in certain shows, which allows me time to be with our children and to pursue other passions.

And you know what? This job, too, provides our health insurance, as well as a regular paycheck. In addition, Carey now owns part of the business—which has been successful, unlike many start-up companies. Is God amazing, or what?

Helen Keller once said, "Security is mostly a superstition. . . . Avoiding danger is no safer in the long run than outright exposure. Life is either a daring adventure, or nothing."

I want my life to count for something—to be a daring adventure. The past five years have stretched my faith and shown me the power of a dream and of God's perfect plans. I've learned that He—not a paycheck or a house or a church—is our security.

And that's a good thing to know in these uncertain times.

Notes from the Coach

He who fears the Lord has a secure fortress,
and for his children it will be a refuge.

Proverbs 14:26 NIV

You get us ready for life: you probe for our soft spots,
you knock off our rough edges.
And I'm feeling so fit, so safe: made right, kept right.
God in solemn honor does things right.

Psalm 7:9–11 MSG

"So I tell you, don't worry about everyday life—
whether you have enough food, drink, and clothes.
Doesn't life consist of more than food and clothing?
Look at the birds. They don't need to plant or harvest or put
food in barns because your heavenly Father feeds them.
And you are far more valuable to him than they are....
And why worry about your clothes? Look at the lilies
and how they grow. They don't work or make their clothing,
yet Solomon in all his glory was not dressed as beautifully
as they are. And if God cares so wonderfully for flowers
that are here today and gone tomorrow, won't he more
surely care for you? You have so little faith!...
Your heavenly Father already knows all your needs,
and he will give you all you need from day to day if you live for
him and make the Kingdom of God your primary concern."

Matthew 6:25–26, 28–30, 32–33 NLT

Leaving a Legacy

*If you cannot get rid of the family skeleton,
at least make him dance.*

GEORGE BERNARD SHAW

Sometimes I wonder—what kind of example am I leaving my children? What will they write on my tombstone or say about me after I'm gone? Maybe "totally absentminded—but beloved mother." Or "she never dusted, but at least she loved us."

I know that I want my children to remember less of my faults—I'm no June Cleaver, that's for sure—and more of my heart. Besides God and my hubby, they are my priorities. So I hope I'm leaving them lots of love.

As for my family tree, I have been given a wonderful legacy of creativity and Christianity. Those are things I want to pass on, as well.

Just what is a legacy? My friend Wendy, who has been given an artistic legacy from her musician parents, says it's the "mark you leave on other people." I think that's a great definition. Legacies can be musical (Natalie Cole), political (the Kennedys), financial (the Rockefellers), or spiritual.

"Legacies are more than warm-and-fuzzy nostalgia," says author Bob Welch in *Where Roots Grow Deep: Stories of Family, Love, and Legacy.* "They guide us. More importantly, they show us, without robbing us of our individual bents, how to act."

Just as it is now becoming important to know our family

medical history—our health's building blocks—since it can help doctors determine risk factors and preventive measures, it is imperative that we examine our past and recognize the building blocks of our faith.

Think back to those who laid the foundation for your spiritual identity. Were your immediate family members role models for your burgeoning Christianity? Or did you find inspiration in friends, pastors, Sunday school teachers, or mentors? Maybe it's time to write them a note and thank them for their contribution to your life.

What about those of us who have black marks on our family legacies? Do we ignore them or sweep them under the proverbial rug? No, for even negative legacies can teach us something.

Wendy's mother spent her life without a spiritual compass. Wendy remembers growing up without faith or a church home—in fact, she was most at home backstage at the symphony concerts her mother played in. But when Wendy met her future husband, Russ, she saw someone with a confidence in Christ that she longed for. Her father had died of cancer, and her mother's death followed soon after. "Russ was the first person I met who was an authentic Christian," she says. "I was drawn to his peaceful spirit and his love for other people."

Because she grew up without a spiritual compass, Wendy is now sensitive to those who don't feel comfortable in typical church settings. And she will pass on to her children that living with faith means "you can't always control what happens to you, but you can control what you do about it."

I love Wendy's attitude. And I think I'll teach my kids that, too.

And hopefully, my epitaph will read something like this: "She hated folding laundry but liked to fold us in her arms."

Notes from the Coach

O my people, hear my teaching;
listen to the words of my mouth.
I will open my mouth in parables,
I will utter hidden things, things from of old—
what we have heard and known,
what our fathers have told us.
We will not hide them from their children;
we will tell the next generation
the praiseworthy deeds of the LORD,
his power, and the wonders he has done.
He decreed statutes for Jacob
and established the law in Israel,
which he commanded our forefathers
to teach their children,
so the next generation would know them,
even the children yet to be born,
and they in turn would tell their children.
Then they would put their trust in God and
would not forget his deeds
but would keep his commands.

PSALM 78:1–7 NIV

A good life gets passed on to the grandchildren.

PROVERBS 13:22 MSG

180

The Sanctity of Simple Things

Teach us delight in simple things.

RUDYARD KIPLING

As I've written before, I've battled depression for several years. Mostly, it's under control because of my medication, exercise, periodic visits to a counselor, family support, and other things I try to make a part of daily life.

One of those "helps" is being grateful for the small miracles that happen every day. Depression can be a black cloud looming over my head, and noticing everyday wonders has helped poke holes in the clouds to let God's grace shine through.

Case in point: a day last spring, which I recorded in my journal—not because of its hugeness, but because of the little things that made it wonderful.

On that particular day, I ached with tiredness, and I had run out of my antidepressants over the weekend and had to wait to get more. (My depression is always worse when I'm tired.) Jordan, Carey, and I were also fighting spring sniffles, which made us all a little testy.

But it was a bright, cloudless afternoon, and Carey decided to mow our backyard, since the height of the grass could have concealed a small car. Jordan helped Carey clean up the toys and play tools strewn about in the backyard. He even put on a half-face mask like Carey, who has to be careful with his allergies when he does yard work. I watched from the table and chairs on the patio, journal and Dr. Pepper beside me.

Then sleepy Jordan asked me if he could have his sleeping bag and put it in his clubhouse so he could "west."

Pretty soon, my four-year-old prince was curled up on his blue and yellow bag, arm around his stuffed frog, fast asleep. No doubt he had been lulled by the sun, the hum of the mower, and the frequent birdsong.

And instead of aching with tiredness and gloominess, I began to ache with love and joy and thankfulness. In our small corner of the universe, I was suddenly bursting with gratitude for small miracles—and large ones. For sniffly boys who sleep contentedly in clubhouses, for hardworking daddies who care for exhausted mommies, for the red bird that kept circling the yard, for blue skies—and for peace.

In that moment, the sanctity of simple things overwhelmed me. It's what Arthur Gordon summed up so well in his lovely book, *A Touch of Wonder*: "In moments of discouragement, defeat, or even despair, there are always certain things to cling to. Little things, usually: remembered laughter, the face of a sleeping child, a tree in the wind—in fact, any reminder of something deeply felt or dearly loved."

There have been many other days when God has brought me peace with little, but important, treasures in the midst of a dark mood. But I've found that it's up to me to recognize them and to not let them float away before whispering, "Thanks." Otherwise, I'll have turned away a precious gift.

As Gordon says, "No man is so poor as not to have many of these small candles. When they are lighted, darkness goes away. . .and a touch of wonder remains."

"Who despises the day of small things?"

Zechariah 4:10 NIV

There are four small creatures,
wisest of the wise they are—
ants—frail as they are,
get plenty of food in for the winter;
marmots—vulnerable as they are,
manage to arrange for rock-solid homes;
locusts—leaderless insects,
yet they strip the field like an army regiment;
lizards—easy enough to catch,
but they sneak past vigilant palace guards.

Proverbs 30:24–28 MSG

Better is a little with the fear of the Lord
Than great treasure and turmoil with it.

Proverbs 15:16 NASB

Boys Will Be Boys

Sometimes I wonder if men and women
really suit each other.
Perhaps they should live next door
and just visit now and then.

KATHARINE HEPBURN

Do you ever find yourself burning with questions that have no answers? Such as:

How can a boy who effortlessly opens restricted e-mail files have trouble closing the toilet lid?

Why do men and boys always "flick" the remote control at the *exact moment* we women become interested in a program?

How can men live with dirty socks strewn all over the house but get upset if there's one empty ice tray in the freezer?

And, most importantly: Why is it that men and women are so different?

God did create us different—for a reason. It only takes a visit to a coed preschool classroom to shoot down the theory that boys and girls are alike. In one class I helped with, the boys gulped down their snacks, slapped their crafts together, and proceeded to turn blocks into guns—all within five minutes. The girls ate slowly, crafted their projects with utmost care, and then played "store" and "house."

I think life would be pretty strange, and downright sad, if both sexes were alike. Imagine if your husband were like your best girlfriend—only when he borrowed your clothes they came back all stretched out!

But how do we survive daily living with other human beings (namely, men) who sometimes seem out to get us? As one of my favorite T-shirts says, "This marriage [or family] was made in heaven—but so was thunder and lightning!"

One thing I've learned is to look for ways I'm similar to the boys in my life and build upon those. As I've pondered those things that drew my hubby and I together when we were dating (shared talents, values, and a love of enormous amounts of popcorn consumed while viewing old *Andy Griffith* reruns), I've tried to rekindle those "sparks" as often as possible.

And though I don't enjoy some of things my sons do, I try to stop what I'm doing and enthusiastically partake in their passions when they ask me to. It's an honor to be asked, and I know it won't happen forever!

I also firmly believe we should affirm men in their uniqueness. Our high-speed, high-achievement culture puts enormous pressure on their shoulders, and criticism only adds to the load. A hug or a kiss can be just the ticket to letting them know we appreciate them.

I'm blessed to have a husband who shares my faith and my values. He's also wonderfully romantic and faithfully supports my own dreams and goals. My sons are affectionate, creative, smart, and hilarious. I could go on, but you get the idea. Now, if I can just say these things out loud once in a while, I'll be on the right track.

So now I have a few more questions:

When was the last time you affirmed your husband or son? If your hairstyle was completely different the last time a compliment came out of your mouth, the time is ripe to say—out loud!—the nice things you've been thinking.

How long has it been since you participated in their passions, without complaining about the sweat, dirt, or broken fingernails involved?

And, most importantly: Do you know a good place to hide the remote control?

NOTES FROM THE COACH

Since we live by the Spirit,
let us keep in step with the Spirit.
Let us not become conceited,
provoking and envying each other.

GALATIANS 5:25–26 NIV

With each of you we were like a father with his child,
holding your hand, whispering encouragement,
showing you step by step how to live well before God,
who called us into his own kingdom, into this delightful life.

1 THESSALONIANS 2:11–12 MSG

Do not let any unwholesome talk come out
of your mouths, but only what is helpful for
building others up according to their needs,
that it may benefit those who listen.
And do not grieve the Holy Spirit of God. . . .
Get rid of all bitterness, rage and anger,
brawling and slander, along with every form of malice.
Be kind and compassionate to one another,
forgiving each other, just as in Christ God forgave you.

EPHESIANS 4:29–32 NIV

1 Corinthians 13 for Busy Moms

Love accepts the trying things of life
without asking for explanations.
It trusts and is at rest.

AMY CARMICHAEL

If I speak in the language of monsters and monkeys when reading bedtime stories, but have not love, I'm like a phone ringing just as we sit down to the dinner table.

If I have the gift of prophecy and know exactly when my husband is going to be late so I can pop dinner in the oven at the precise moment he leaves work, but have not love, I am nothing.

If I can chase a naked toddler through the house while listening to voice mail, but don't have love, it profits me nothing.

Love is patient while watching and praying by the front window when it's thirty minutes past curfew.

Love is kind when our teen says, "I hate you!" after we've told him he can't go to a party.

Love does not brag when other parents share their disappointments and insecurities, and love rejoices when other families succeed.

It doesn't boast, even when I've multitasked all day long, and my hubby has trouble reading the paper without falling asleep.

Love does not envy the neighbor's swimming pool or their brand-new minivan, but trusts the Lord to provide all we need. Besides, who has the body for a swimming pool, anyway?

It is not rude when my spouse innocently asks, "What have you done today?" with that tone of voice that implies I've done nothing all day but watch soaps and eat bonbons.

It does not seek after glory immediately when we see talent in our child, because we know that no matter how good he is, the ability to play the national anthem under his armpit will probably not yield a recording contract. Love encourages him to get training and make wise choices.

Love is not easily angered, even when your fifteen-year-old acts like the world revolves around her.

It always protects our children's self-esteem and spirit, even while doling out discipline. It always trusts God to protect our children when we cannot. It always perseveres, through Britney Spears, blue nail polish, burps and other bodily functions, rolled eyes and crossed arms, messy rooms and sleepovers.

Love never fails.

But where there are memories of thousands of diaper changes and painful labor, they will fade away.

Where there is talking back, it will—eventually—cease. (Please, Lord?)

Where there is a teenager who thinks she knows everything, there will come an adult who knows you did your best.

For we know we fail our children, and we pray that they don't end up in therapy. But when we get to heaven, our imperfect parenting will disappear. (Thank God!)

When we were children, we needed a parent to love and protect us. Now that we're parents ourselves, we have a heavenly Father who adores us, shelters us, and holds us when we need to cry.

And now these three remain: faith, hope, and love.

But the greatest of these is. . .a mother's love.

Notes from the Coach

For we know in part and we prophesy in part,
but when perfection comes,
the imperfect disappears.
When I was a child, I talked like a child,
I thought like a child,
I reasoned like a child. When I became a man,
I put childish ways behind me.
Now we see but a poor reflection as in a mirror;
then we shall see face to face.
Now I know in part;
then I shall know fully, even as I am fully known.
And now these three remain: faith, hope and love.
But the greatest of these is love.

1 Corinthians 13:9–13 niv

Get along among yourselves,
each of you doing your part....
Gently encourage the stragglers,
and reach out for the exhausted,
pulling them to their feet.
Be patient with each person,
attentive to individual needs.
And be careful that when you get on
each other's nerves you don't snap at each other.
Look for the best in each other,
and always do your best to bring it out.

1 Thessalonians 5:13–15 msg

Sources

Barbour Publishing, Inc., expresses its appreciation to all those who generously gave permission to reprint copyrighted material. Diligent effort has been made to identify, locate, contact, and secure permission to use copyrighted material. If any permissions or acknowledgments have been inadvertently omitted or if such permissions were not received by the time of publication, the publisher would sincerely appreciate receiving complete information so that correct credit can be given in future editions.

Albom, Mitch. *The Five People You Meet in Heaven.* New York: Hyperion, 2003. Excerpt on page 31 used by permission.

Bolander, Varner, Greene, and Wright, comp. Instant Quotation Dictionary. Mundelein, IL: Career Publishing, 1969.

BrainyQuote Web site—http://www.brainyquote.com. Brainy Media, 2003.

Gire, Ken. *Windows of the Soul: Experiencing God in New Ways.* Grand Rapids, MI: Zondervan, 1996. Excerpt on page 38 used by permission.

Gordon, Arthur. *A Touch of Wonder.* Grand Rapids, MI: Baker/Revell, 1974. Excerpts on pages 167 and 182 used by permission.

Hosier, Helen, comp. *The Quotable Christian: Favorite Quotes from Notable Christians.* Uhrichsville, OH: Barbour Publishing, 1998.

Johnson, Nicole. *Fresh-Brewed Life: A Stirring Invitation to Wake Up Your Soul.* Nashville: Thomas Nelson, 1999. Excerpts on pages 91 and 109 used by permission of Thomas Nelson. All rights reserved.

Kephart, Beth. *Into the Tangle of Friendship: A Memoir of the Things That Matter.* New York: Houghton Mifflin, 2000. Excerpt on pages 130–131 used by permission.

Lamott, Anne. *Traveling Mercies: Some Thoughts on Faith.* New York: Random House/Pantheon, 1999. Excerpt on pages 58–59 used by permission.

Mason, Mike. *The Mystery of Children: What Our Kids Teach Us about Childlike Faith.* Colorado Springs: WaterBrook Press, 2001. Excerpt on page 68 used by permission of WaterBrook Press. All rights reserved.

Meyers, Jan. *The Allure of Hope: God's Pursuit of a Woman's Heart.* Colorado Springs: NavPress, 2001. Excerpt on page 147 used by permission.

Moore, Edwin, ed. *Collins Quotation Finder.* Glasgow, Scotland: HarperCollins, 2001.

Partner, Daniel, ed. *Heroes of the Faith: Memorable Quotes from Men and Women of Faith.* Uhrichsville, OH: Barbour Publishing, 1998.

Reader's Digest Quotable Quotes: Wit and Wisdom for All Occasions from America's Most Popular Magazine. Pleasantville, NY: Reader's Digest Association, 1997.

Webb, Rhonda Rizzo. *Words Begin in Our Hearts: What God Says about What We Say.* Chicago: Moody Publishers, 2003. Excerpts on pages 169–170 used by permission of Moody Publishers. All rights reserved.

Welch, Bob. *Where Roots Grow Deep: Stories of Family, Love, and Legacy.* Eugene, OR: Harvest House, 1999. Excerpt on page 178 used by permission. All rights reserved.

About the Author

Dena Dyer's favorite roles are that of wife to Carey and mom to their boys, Jordan and Jackson. Her other roles include professional actress and singer, women's speaker, and author. Dena has written for publication since the age of twelve and has credits in hundreds of magazines, such as *Woman's World, Today's Christian Woman, Writer's Digest, Christian Reader,* and *Discipleship Journal.* She has also contributed to several anthologies. When she has free time (grin!), Dena enjoys participating in the women's and music ministries at her church, scrapbooking, watching old movies, and decorating. For more information, visit her Web site: www.denadyer.com.